55 Surefire

FOOD-RELATED BUSINESSES

You Can Start for *Under $5,000*

The Surefire Series

55 Surefire Food Businesses You Can Start for Under $5000

55 Surefire Internet Businesses You Can Start for Under $5000

55 Surefire Homebased Businesses You Can Start for Under $5000

SUREFIRE

Entrepreneur
MAGAZINE'S

55 Surefire
FOOD-RELATED
BUSINESSES
You Can Start for *Under $5,000*

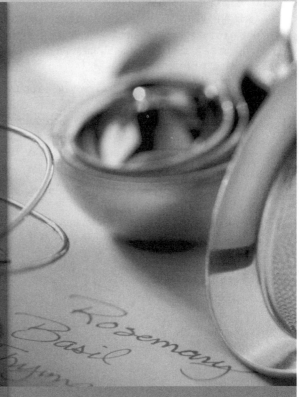

Catering • Wedding Cakes • Bread Making
• Artisan Cheeses • Food Writer • Cooking
Classes • Maple Syrup Production/Sales •
Picnic Baskets • BBQ • Hot Dog Cart • Meals-
to-Go • Gourmet Popcorn • Herb Sales •
Bartender • Coffee Cart • Lunch Wagon
• Cookware Sales • Winemaking • Gift
Baskets • Personal Chef • Chocolate Making
• Vegetable Stand • Pizza Stand • Juice Bar
• Fresh Pasta • Seafood Sales • Gourmet Pet
Foods • Natural Baby Food • Restaurant
Cleaning Service • Food Co-Operative •
Restaurant Equipment Sales • Ice Cream
Stand • and Many More

Entrepreneur Press & Cheryl Kimball

Jere L. Calmes, Publisher
Cover Design: Kaochoy Saeteurn
Composition and Production: MillerWorks

This publication is designed to provide accurate and authoritative information
in regard to the subject matter covered. It is sold with the understanding that the
publisher is not engaged in rendering legal, accounting or other professional services. If legal
advice or other expert assistance is required, the services of a
competent professional person should be sought.

Library of Congress Cataloging-in-Publication Data
Kimball, Cheryl.
55 surefire food-related businesses you can start for under $5,000 / by
Cheryl Kimball and Entrepreneur Press.
    p. cm.
  ISBN 1-59918-255-6 (alk. paper)
    1. Food industry and trade—Management. 2. New business enterprises--
Management. 3. Small business—Management. I. Entrepreneur Press. II. Title. III.
Title: Fifty-five surefire food-related businesses you can start for under $5,000.
HD9000.5.K515 2009   664.0068'1--dc22
2009001619

Printed in Canada

CONTENTS

CONTENTS

PREFACE

I opened a bookstore back in the late '80s, just before the heyday of the New England real estate bust. The store lasted for two-and-one-half years before I closed it, wiser but considerably poorer.

My shop was located on a trendy street on the working waterfront of the trendy little seaside town of Portsmouth, New Hampshire, nestled between the tugboat dock, the scrap iron yard, a popular ice cream shop, and no less than seven fine restaurants. Over those years, my father— who typically never went anywhere he didn't absolutely have to—would surprise me with an occasional visit. He was, in great part, responsible for my love of books and reading, and he seemed to truly like the store. But he never refrained from reminding me that, in his opinion, I could be a lot more successful financially if I sold hot dogs out the side window.

A few years later, my husband and I bought our 200-year-old home with 90 acres and a private beach on a small lake around the corner. My dad thought we could make a killing selling hot dogs from a boat out on the lake. And when we purchased a small cabin on the back corner of our acreage that sat right along a popular snowmobile trail... you guessed it. Dad thought that my fortune could be had selling hot dogs—and perhaps hot chocolate—to the passing snowmobilers.

The funny thing is, after a couple more retailers tried to make a go of it in my old bookstore space, the building owner's son took it over and created a sandwich shop. Yup—hot dogs on the menu. And you guessed it: the sandwich shop is still going strong, far exceeding the two-and-one-half years my bookstore was in business.

People not only need to eat, they love to eat. If you enjoy the food business, one way or another there is a way you can make a living in a food-related enterprise.

So let's get started with the basics before we delve into 55 surefire food businesses for you to consider. Summer is coming and as soon as I am done with this book, I need to get out on the lake and start selling hot dogs to those boaters....

INTRODUCTION

The business of food is a very specialized one, different in many ways from other types of business ventures. Although there are a few businesses in this book that don't work with food directly, the majority do. And it's that food that makes the food business so unique.

TAKING CARE OF BUSINESS

Here are a few things you will need to know about to work with food.

Food Safety

To work with food, you will need to become extremely familiar with food safety standards as mandated by the Food & Drug Administration. There are many websites that you should bookmark on your computer, including:

- FoodSafety.gov, a dissemination site billed as the "Gateway to Government Food Safety Information." Here you will find safety alerts, such as the salmonella outbreak in peanut products that occurred during the writing of this book, and the latest news regarding food safety and handling. This is primarily a consumer-oriented website, but it is well organized and comprehensive.

- fsis.usda.gov, the website for the Food Safety and Inspection Service, is another place to ind the latest news regarding food safety, recalls, and other food-related public health concerns.

- fda.gov is the site for the U.S. Food and Drug Administration. Here you will find a whole section specifically on food. You can register online as a food facility that manufactures, processes, packs, or holds food for either human or animal consumption. There is also information about labeling, packaging, additives, and other guidance.

- usda.gov has a "food and nutrition" section that includes general information on things such as the food pyramid and child nutrition as well as information on food safety, recalls, security issues, and other food-related news.

You should also plan to contact your state and local governments to make sure you know the licensing requirements and regulations you need to follow to start any kind of food-related business in your state or municipality. If you are dealing with liquor on any level, be sure to check with the state's liquor commission and find out what rules you need to follow with regard to liquor sales or consumption.

Labeling and Packaging

When you create food products, you need to consider labeling and packaging from both marketing and regulatory standpoints. The government has all sorts of rules and regulations you need to follow when it comes to labeling, so make sure you have a thorough understanding of what is required for your particular product.

From a presentation standpoint, you should consider several things:

- The label should be attractive and clearly describe what the customer is buying

- The label design should be in keeping with the marketing style you want your business to convey

- The packaging should be attractive and convenient to the consumer.

Both packaging and labeling should be appealing and effective, but don't get carried away and create something unnecessarily expensive whose costs will need to be passed along to the consumer. Unless there is an obvious benefit to consumers, they don't want to pay for labeling and packaging excesses; they want to pay for high-quality food.

Presentation

Presentation is a term typically reserved for the way a chef places the food on a plate before it is served to the customer. Colors, textures, portion size, garnishes are all taken into consideration. But presentation is important in any type of food-related business (or any business for that matter).

If you are running a roadside vegetable stand, using wooden baskets to display your produce is more attractive and fitting than putting it in plastic containers. Enticing office workers to buy the nuts you have for sale is easier if they are neatly arranged in plastic tubs and not tossed randomly in a cardboard box. It not only looks better to have a nice presentation, it sells better.

Perishables

One of the most difficult aspects of the food business is dealing with food that is perishable. With time, you will become increasingly skilled at estimating what you will need and will waste less. But in the beginning, it may become quite stressful as you throw away food products; it certainly isn't good for the bottom line! But, rest assured, you will become better at it. And to increase your proficiency from the start, learn as much as you can about projecting your needs. Chances are if you are going into the food business, you have worked in the food business for someone else. Pick their brains as much as possible about how to estimate inventory purchases to give yourself a running start with wasting as little food as possible.

Truth in Advertising

As mentioned earlier, you need to be cognizant of the regulations regarding labeling of food products. This includes being exacting about what is in your product; if it is salsa, for instance, be sure to list every ingredient. Not only is this the law, but there are serious concerns regarding food allergies that can be dangerous to some people. Peanuts have become widely known as a serious allergen for children, for instance; today it seems every food vendor whose product has even just been driven by a place that uses peanuts notes that on the label. You also want to indicate how the product is cooked: If you are selling homemade tortilla chips, for example, be sure to indicate whether they are baked or deep fried.

The trust between consumer and manufacturer innately includes the consumer's trust that the manufacturer is truthful and forthcoming about every aspect of the food product.

HOW THIS BOOK IS ORGANIZED

In the following pages you will find 55 food-related businesses to consider in your search for the right business to start. Each business idea starts with some opening information, including a little about the business idea in general, what kind of special education or experience you might need to be successful, and perhaps a couple of different ways you can specialize in that business category. Under each listing, you will also find discussions on the following topics.

Things to Consider

This section is intended to point out less obvious factors about the specific business—such as how hard it is to be successful in a particular business unless you have worked in the industry and start with a list of potential clients. Or that you will need a lot of inventory storage space. This section also covers points such as whether the business is particularly physically demanding and the like.

How Do You Want to Spend Your Day?

This is something many people don't think through quite enough until they are already committed to what they thought was a good idea. What do you consider the perfect day? One where you are done with work by noon? One where you are on your feet most of the time or sitting at a desk most of the time? One where you can lock yourself in your office and be alone doing research or one where you are interacting with people most of the day?

The great thing about being in business for yourself is you are often free to get up and take the dog for a walk or sit with the kids and share an after-school snack or generally stretch your legs and clear your head any time you want. But if you are starting your own business, you will also have to work hard to get it up and running; it pays in the long run to be clear about what your best day looks like and find a business that fits into that as closely as possible.

What You Will Need

Almost all businesses these days require a computer workstation, even if it is just to keep your records and bookkeeping up to date. But many businesses have special requirements. Those will be listed, including special vehicle or storage needs.

Marketing Angle

Every business needs to be marketed. There are some general marketing approaches that work for all businesses, but then each business has its own individual marketing angle. This short section will give you some idea of what you will have to do for marketing in order to not only get your business up and running, but how to keep it successful.

Nice Touch

This section will give you some ideas on how you can go the extra mile with your customers to give them a lasting positive impression of you and your business and services. Whether it's a frequent-buyer card or a free dessert with your meal, these are the kinds of things that will have customers telling their friends and family about your business.

Expansion Possibilities

Most businesses can start out modestly and expand into other areas when they are ready to grow the business, especially when starting up a business for under $5,000. This section will provide a couple of ideas of where you might be able to grow in the future once you have an established track record and perhaps working capital.

Words to Know

As you learn about a business idea, there are some words associated with that business that you will need to know in order to understand the underlying concepts. Each business's mini glossary explains two or three terms you might encounter as you explore the idea further. The glossary is by no means extensive, but just a taste of some of the terminology.

Resources

Lastly, each business idea is accompanied by helpful resources; mostly websites, but some trade magazines as well. These are not intended as endorsements of companies or products, but instead offer an opportunity for you to get more information, find a supplier, or simply to look at other similar businesses to get a better sense of what you might be getting yourself into.

IN GENERAL

No matter what business you decide to start, there are some general things that are common to all businesses. And there are a few things that are assumed in order to keep your start-up business within the "less than $5,000" criteria promised in the title.

Vehicles

This is probably the biggest concern when keeping your business's costs under $5,000. Needless to say, if a business requires a van or truck to haul equipment, that vehicle will cost more than $5,000. These days, it would be difficult to find even a well-used vehicle of that nature for under $5,000—and even if the purchase price meets that criteria, you would still probably have to put that much into it again just to make it road worthy.

The assumption here is that you will either already own an appropriate vehicle or will lease it. Leasing often requires a small down payment, if any, and the monthly lease payment can probably be written off on your taxes as a business expense (be sure to check with your tax accountant on that and any other tax information). There are a couple of advantages to leasing:

- It offers you a way into the business without having to purchase an expensive vehicle
- You can trade the vehicle in at the end of the lease and either buy it or another vehicle at that time or lease a new vehicle.

There are also a couple disadvantages:

- By leasing, you have no equity in the vehicle
- If you decide to get out of your business before the end of the lease period, you may pay a penalty for returning the vehicle before

the lease is over. Check the fine print on this or see whether you can sublease the vehicle for the remainder of the lease period if necessary.

Business Cards

Always carry business cards with you. If you have a computer (see "Basic Computer Workstation" later in this section), you can create business cards easily and inexpensively. Many word-processing programs enable you to create business cards by choosing a template you like and plugging in your business information. You then purchase perforated business card stock and print out ten to a sheet.

Include your business name, your name, business address, phone number, fax number, e-mail address, and website address on the business card. If your business name is self-explanatory, or if there is room for a short sell line on the card—"Low-fat chips you will love"—it can double as an ad posted on community bulletin boards.

Advertising

You need to plan to do some advertising; it's that simple. It doesn't have to be extensive or complicated, but if you are serious about your business, you need to have its name out there. Even if it's just a small display ad in the weekly free newspaper, be sure you include in your start-up capital enough funds to keep that going. Multiple impressions are how your ad is going to make an impact. Readers of the paper may not need restaurant cleaning services or fresh produce right now, but when they do, they will remember that they've seen your ad several times in the paper.

Create a Website

These days, almost everyone goes to the internet for information about a service or product they need. Be sure that they find you when they are searching for what you have to offer. And creating a website does not have to be difficult or complicated. Register a domain name through one of the popular sites such as GoDaddy.com. Then create a basic website. Many internet service providers offer free website templates. Pay the small monthly fee to a hosting service to keep it up and running. Add a blog to give website visitors added value. Learn a little bit about search engine optimization so that when surfers search the web using words that relate to your business, your website will appear on the first or second page of matches.

If you start with something simple, you can build and change your website as you go along, which will keep people interested in coming back. At the very least, it will give them the basic information they need to contact.

A Business Is a Business

Even though you are starting your business on a shoestring budget, always treat your business like a business. Expect to get adequately and fairly compensated for the work you do or the product you sell. Be careful to charge for all supplies. Get the appropriate insurance coverage to protect your assets. And act professionally at all times.

Write a Business Plan

Part of always treating your business like a business is to create a business plan. This detailed document can be simply for your own purposes to help you to better understand and organize your business, to help you plan for the long term or for expansion, or for presentation to a financial institution to gain start-up or expansion funding.

A business plan consists of:

- An overview of your business

- Market research of the general business climate in this industry in your area, including any competing businesses
- A marketing plan that shows how you are going to advertise and promote your business and attract customers
- Background information about you, including your resume, and include similar information about any key employees or partners
- Financial statements, at least including a personal income statement, start-up expenses, and pro forma profit-and-loss statements month-by-month for one year and another one at three-years.
- Any sample contracts or other legal documents that relate to the business, such as equipment leasing contracts.

If you take the time to write a thorough business plan, you may be surprised how many times you refer to this document in your first year of business.

Basic Computer Workstation

Almost any business you undertake will require at least a basic computer and peripherals. You should plan to have the following:

- **A desktop computer.** A PC-based computer, equipped with the latest Pentium processor, 320-500GB of hard drive memory, 2-3GB of short-term memory, and the ability to burn DVDs and CDs, will cost approximately $500. Apple's iMac, an all-in-one desktop package, runs about $1000.

- **Large-screen monitor.** These days, you can get a TV-like flat-panel monitor for your PC CPU for around $200. Look for high resolution (1440 x 900) and good contrast (500:1).

- **Accessories.** Unless you buy a desktop package with everything included in the box (approximately $1,000), you will also need to purchase a keyboard and a mouse. If the business you are starting requires you to be on the computer a lot, save your wrists and buy an ergonomic keyboard; once you get used to it, you will never have another. Most any mouse will do; pick the one that feels best in your hand. You can also choose to go wireless on both of these accessories and keep your desk a little less cluttered.

- **Connections.** Check that your PC comes with all the necessary cords. You will need to connect the monitor to electric service and to the computer CPU. You will need an electrical cord for the CPU. Keyboards usually come with a built-in cord to plug into the CPU.

- **Internet service.** Sign on with an internet service provider. If dial-up is all you can afford or all that is available in your area, so be it. Otherwise, skip this slow and often inconvenient approach and go straight to high-speed internet access through your phone or cable service. The difference is worth every penny.

- **Wireless internet connection.** If you choose to use a laptop computer as your main computer, you may want to get wireless internet access. It can cost you more per month in service fees, and you will need yet another piece of equipment, known as a router, to receive the wireless connection and send it around your immediate area. You may even require yet another piece of equipment, a booster, if the area in which you wish to have internet access is large or has obstructions such as building walls. But if being able to move around your place of business with your laptop is important, then by all means consider wireless internet. Otherwise, you will need a modem (usually provided by the ISP) and a cable long enough to reach from the modem to your desktop.

You will also need some other computer-run machines, known as "peripherals." These might include:

- **Printer.** A printer is a must. Printers have gone up in quality and down in price. If you will be using your printer primarily to print invoices and statements, you can get away with a basic printer with a price tag of less than $200. If your business calls for product information sheets, photos of any kind, or other printed material to be given to customers, consider a higher-quality printer. You can choose between inkjet and laser, both of which run anywhere from $150-$500. The inks and toners can cost more in a year's time than the machine itself!

- **Scanner.** A scanner allows you to scan photos and text and put them in digitized form. Scanners are so inexpensive—less that $200—that depending how often you might use one, they can be worth having around.

- **Fax machine.** While not run by your computer per se, you should definitely own a fax machine. You practically can't find a standalone fax machine anymore, but if you do, it won't cost more than $100.

- **All-in-One.** The latest craze is for all-in-one machines that include a scanner, printer, and fax machine as well as the ability to print photos directly from your digital camera or the camera's memory card all in one machine about the size of a regular printer. These seem pretty handy, and they do make sense when you consider that all of these functions operate in pretty much the same way. However, if something fundamental breaks down on the machine, or one component needs repairs and you are without the machine for a week or so, you are without all of these functions! For some businesses, that may not be a big issue, so these all-in-one machines are excellent choices. For others, it is not the best choice and getting separate machines for each function is the better route.

- **Digital camera,** Lastly, any business will benefit from having a digital camera. You can use it to take product shots for your website or eBay. You can take photos of your finished jobs to put on your website or to add to marketing materials. The uses of a digital camera are myriad. They are available with a wide range of prices and options, but high-quality digital cameras have come down in price in recent years; for example, a 10-megapixel Canon Digital Rebel SLR is now around $600.

HAPPY HUNTING

That's all the equipment you need to get started! Now you can go ahead and pick your food-related business. There are 55 great ideas that include both the most fundamental food-related businesses as well as some unique ones—at least a few of which surely have your name on them!

ICON KEY

$	=	$1500 or less to startup
$$	=	$1500 - $3000 to startup
$$$	=	$3000 - $5000 to startup
	=	Some experience, special training and/or licencing may be needed
	=	has great expansion possibilities

CATERING

1

The catering business is multi-faceted. To keep it below the $5,000 limit mandated by this book, you will want to keep your startup simple. The best way to do that is to find a focus for your catering business. Don't worry, you can always branch out later. But zeroing in on one type of catering can get you started and help you build the capital you need to expand.

The possibilities are endless. You can start a catering business that specializes in

- birthday parties for kids
- the traditional lobster/clam bake
- wedding catering
- special-event catering for birthdays, anniversaries, graduations, and homecomings
- the corporate market
- holiday catering, particularly Thanksgiving and Christmas

The best way to start and expand in the catering business is to approach your business from a seasonal perspective. Opening as a lobster-bake business, for example, can keep you busy through the summer months and well into the fall, but winds down in time for you to plan for the holiday catering.

As with so many businesses, the corporate market can be where you make the most money as a caterer. But it comes with a price as well.

First, you need to be sure you can handle the size of a corporate catering business. Many startup businesses of all kinds have gone wide-eyed into a market that is bigger than they can handle only to find that instead of being the financial boon they thought it would be, it actually put them under. Get your feet wet with smaller companies whose events you can handle without having to expand your employees and equipment to the stretching point.

Also, you may need to gain a bit of a reputation before you can adequately market yourself to the corporate world. In the meantime, scout out groups and post flyers to attract local catering jobs such as the gardening club or the volunteer appreciation event for the local historical museum. These people all work in different places and have family and friends who can provide a large word-of-mouth network when they relate what a great meal they had.

If you have a specialty that you enjoy, revolve your startup around that. It may be something that all your friends insist you make and bring to any party to which you are invited. For a startup, having a signature dish or menu can be very good for business. Perhaps it is vegetarian sushi, or 25 different chicken dishes, it doesn't matter as long as it gets people talking.

THINGS TO CONSIDER

You will want to be logical in what you choose for a catering business if you plan to expand later. It would be more difficult to become known for children's birthday parties and then try to expand into wedding catering. It can be done, but it may not be the best approach.

Also, don't forget to name your business something logical for that future expansion. Again, a company named "Parties for the Potty-Trained" isn't going to fly when you try to market yourself as a wedding caterer.

HOW DO YOU WANT TO SPEND YOUR DAY?

As a caterer, your schedule is at the whim of your clients. This most likely means a lot of Friday and Saturday nights and other weekend work. Make sure this works for you. If your spouse works nine to five, Monday through Friday, you are not going to see much of her or him—unless, of course, she or he is keen on helping you in the business!

You need to be willing to spend a lot of time with strangers who are having a good time all around you. But spending most of your time at parties sounds like it can be a good thing!

WHAT YOU WILL NEED

If you start out modestly, your needs are modest. You won't need a commercial size kitchen, for example. Or even a commercial oven, although that would be nice.

There are two types of things you will need: behind-the-scenes cookware and serving dishes and utensils. Starter cookware might include:

- large pots for making things such as soups, stews, and sauces

- large frying pans to pre-brown meats

- large baking pans for making things such as lasagna and casseroles —don't buy pans that are larger than your oven!

- outdoor cooking gear; if you are doing barbeques and the like, you will need a grill, grill tools, and fuel.

Keep in mind that many of the places where special events take place have cooking facilities including some or, perhaps, all necessities. Some basic serving equipment includes:

- chafing dishes that allow you to keep food covered and warm with low heat

- attractive serving pieces for cold dishes, such as salads

- serving utensils: spoons, forks, tongs. Buy several of each of these and either mark them or buy unique ones that are identical. These kinds of small items disappear easily.

- tablecloths to cover large serving tables

- depending on your focus, you may need some specialized items such as flowers for the serving table, piñatas for a Cinco de Mayo party, or holiday decor for a Christmas party.

You will need a vehicle in this business. If you start off modestly, the vehicle doesn't need to be a cargo van; even a hatchback will probably suffice. If you don't have something appropriate to get started, check into leasing a vehicle.

MARKETING ANGLE

Use that specialty that you are known for among your friends to market your catering business. And market your theme—lobster bakes, kids' parties—whatever it is. But don't create marketing materials that completely limit your ability to adapt the materials as you expand.

Cleanliness is key in the food business. Make sure everything about your business makes a neat and tidy impression, from the brochures you post to the tablecloths you put on the serving table.

NICE TOUCH

Acknowledge your customers' special events. If you are catering a 50th-anniversary party, bring a gift for the happy couple—something modest and simple, such as a set of golden candles. At the very least, take a moment to introduce yourself and wish them well. As the caterer, you become part of the party. You don't need to dance and sit down and eat with the guests; that would be inappropriate. But acknowledging the special occasion in a small way will have guests remarking how considerate you are.

EXPANSION POSSIBILITIES

The catering world is huge; start small and the expansion possibilities are endless. Keep in mind what kind of catering you most like to do; if you don't enjoy kids, don't start a birthday party business!

WORDS TO KNOW

Cross Contamination: A transfer of bacteria from one surface to another. An example of cross contamination is to use a cutting board to cut meat and then use the same cutting board without properly sanitizing it to cut vegetables. Bacteria in the raw meat will be killed when the meat is cooked to appropriate temperatures, but if the vegetables are going to be used for raw appetizers, any bacteria that crossed from the meat to the veggies will not be killed and could cause illness.

Food Pyramid: The USDA standard for nutritious eating. The pyramid consists of recommended percentages of grains, vegetables, fruits, dairy products, and meat and beans for a healthy diet. Be sure you consider these five categories when you prepare your catering menus.

Kosher: Jewish laws that govern how food must be sold, served, and used. If you want to offer kosher catering, you need to understand these strict guidelines.

RESOURCES

ascateringsupplies.com
cateringsupplies.com

WEDDING CAKES

Creativity in wedding cakes has gone to a whole new level. This can be a fun and exciting business for which you become well known and the go-to baker when it comes to wedding cakes in your area.

One of your biggest concerns in the wedding cake business is how to get the cake safely to the reception site. Check ahead to find out where the delivery should be made, if anyone will be there to let you in, and if there is a table set up and ready for the cake. If it is 110 degrees in the shade, you don't want to leave the cake in your vehicle while you look for the person with the key and wait for someone to find and set up a table.

If you will need to retrieve things such as platters and construction elements, you might also offer to provide the table so you know a table will be available. Be sure the table is big enough to hold not only the cake, but also a stack of plates, forks, and cocktail napkins, as well as some pieces of cut cake.

You may want to consider hiring a part-time assistant. This person can help when two sets of hands are needed, can be available when you have one of those busier-than-usual days, and can help with deliveries.

THINGS TO CONSIDER

People will want to taste your cakes before they ordering. Make small cakes once or twice a week that can be offered to potential clients. You can sell them at a small price that is deducted from the client's bill if a wedding cake is ordered from you. If the client decides not to order, you will have at least covered your costs.

HOW DO YOU WANT TO SPEND YOUR DAY?

Baking wedding cakes is a good business for someone who likes to work independently. It is an indoor business that requires your full attention—you may be able to sit on the patio while the cake bakes, but you won't want to take the dog for a walk in the park while there is a cake in the oven. So plan to be indoors a lot. However, you certainly can bake in the evenings and early mornings, so you can have your day to yourself with this business.

While the cake is baking, you will most likely be doing cleanup. Or you can browse magazines and websites to look for new ideas.

You should be able to do this business mostly on weekdays, since most weddings take place on Saturday, with the exception of delivery, which will need to happen the day of the wedding—so plan for a spurt of activity early Saturday mornings.

WHAT YOU WILL NEED

Baking for wedding cakes needn't be expensive. You will need a variety of cake pans, cooling racks, and utensils to move the cake parts. You will also need a variety of decorating tools, including an icing bag and various tips. Start small, however. You can add to your collection at any time for a specific cake; build your equipment as you build your business.

Your biggest investment will be a commercial-grade oven. You could use your regular house oven, but you should be certain it consistently runs at the temperatures you need. And when your business really takes off, you will need a commercial oven to accommodate it.

Ingredients for the individual cakes can be bought with the deposit you will require your customers to provide.

Your personal vehicle should be fine for wedding cake deliveries. However, be sure to create a clean and stable space to transport the cakes. You don't want to show up at a reception site with dog hair all over the cake container. Eventually, you may want to get a vehicle that is more suitable for wedding cake delivery—and one that your employee can use for deliveries—but that can wait until you are much more established.

MARKETING ANGLE

If you decide to make wedding cakes, you may want to branch out into other cakes as well. That's fine, but the wedding market is huge and specific, so you want to establish yourself as a wedding cake baker first. Anniversary cakes are certainly similar, and baking several cakes for large functions is a good way to keep your business going during the months when there are fewer weddings.

NICE TOUCH

Why be like so many bakers and make wedding cakes that look nice but are not good to eat? If yours are beautiful and they also taste great, everyone will be impressed and pass the word.

EXPANSION POSSIBILITIES

As mentioned earlier, you certainly can choose to add other categories of cakes to your repertoire. The wedding industry is so targeted, it is obvious how to market it (although that is not to underestimate that it is also extremely competitive). You may find other markets a little more scattered.

One great way to expand is to provide high-quality restaurants in your market area with a couple of items for their dessert menus. This is also a great way to market your wedding cake business: Ask the restaurant to promote your wedding cake business so that anyone who eats your delicious cake for dessert can remember you when they need a wedding cake.

WORDS TO KNOW

Fondant: A type of cake icing that is a sugar syrup crystallized to be very smooth and creamy.

Oven thermometer: A specialized thermometer uses specifically to measure oven temperature. Always use one. Ovens can be off significantly enough (as much as 75 degrees) to have a big impact on the success of your cakes.

Piping: The act of using an icing tube with a variety of possible tips to decorate the cake.

RESOURCES

cakerysupplies.com

simply-elegant-cakes.com

3 BREADMAKING

Nothing rounds off a meal like a great loaf of bread, and it makes a great gift to bring to a dinner party. If you love to bake, people will definitely pay a high price for an excellent loaf. And what better way to spend your day than taking in the aromas of bread in the oven?

Most people think of bread making as a time-consuming, complicated process. That's where you come in! Your customers will appreciate that good bread can be had by simply buying it from you.

One of your main tasks before your bake your first loaf is to figure out how you are going to sell it. It is unlikely that you live in a place where you can sell a sufficient number of loaves of bread to passersby at the end of your driveway. Is there a large company nearby where you could market your breads, take orders, and supply workers at the end of the day? Or perhaps a place to set up a vending cart? The ideal solution would be to find an outlet that will sell them for you—maybe a local coffee shop, or a shop where the local work force stops at the end of the day.

It will take some time to figure out just how many loaves a day you will need to make. Your market will determine that, but if you have an income goal in mind, you need to decide if you can actually make that number of loaves and if you can find the customers to buy them.

As mentioned in the "Expansion Possibilities" section, you can choose to make breads to supply a restaurant. This is a great way to concentrate your business. But it is better to establish a name for your breads first. That way, the restaurant can promote your breads on their menu as a selling point, and your non-restaurant sales will also expand if the restaurant provides the information diners need to get your breads in the retail arena.

THINGS TO CONSIDER

It is difficult to get big in the breadmaking business without expanding into a commercial space. But just because you have to lease a space to bake your breads doesn't mean you have to be tied down to a retail store. You can still work within a concentrated time frame in which you make the breads. Or maybe each day you have a "day-old" bread sale with an honor box at the front of your baking space. This is especially workable if your workspace has busy foot traffic, although those spaces are usually more expensive to lease than you should plan to spend. But perhaps you can find good space just around the corner from those busy storefronts. And with bread, people can just follow their noses to find you!

HOW DO YOU WANT TO SPEND YOUR DAY?

Baking of any kind requires you to spend long hours on your feet and confined to the kitchen. It can—and probably should—be done in the wee hours of the morning. This doesn't mean the time you spend baking needs to be unpleasant—quite the contrary. Soft music or the news can carry you through your work. If you have to work during hours when nothing is on the radio, consider getting an iPod or some other device that allows you to get podcasts of your favorite radio programs and play them on your own time frame.

WHAT YOU WILL NEED

You will need a commercial-sized oven if you plan to make a go of a breadmaking business. New commercial ovens exceed the $5,000 limit, but you may be able to find a place where you can lease an oven for a year or so. You may find one used at auction, as long as you start looking well before you plan to start your business.

You will also want a commercial mixer and a bread slicer, as well as a supply of bread pans and a cooling rack.

Depending on where you intend to set up your venture, you may need to install some electrical upgrades to run a commercial bread oven. You'll also want a spoons, spatulas, measuring cups, measuring spoons, and other small equipment. And finally, you will need a supply of bread bags in which to sell the loaves.

MARKETING ANGLE

You will definitely want to market your breads to busy people who love good food, but barely have the time to cook dinner, let alone bake their own bread. Make it easy for them to pick up a fresh loaf on their way home from work.

NICE TOUCH

Encourage your customers to buy more by offering them a warm slice of bread when they make a purchase. You can test market new kinds of breads this way: ask them to fill out a quick card to share their response. And this may entice those who hadn't planned to buy anything.

EXPANSION POSSIBILITIES

One way to expand is to offer items other than bread. You can add "quick breads" (those whose dough doesn't need rising), muffins, or perhaps even flavored butters to complement certain breads. However, it is best to become well known for your bread first before diluting your expertise with other baked goods.

Another way to expand is to find a commercial outlet for your breads. Restaurants and local markets are always on the lookout for ways to include local foods on their menus and shelves.

Hire a designer to design a distinctive logo for your bread company. This will help you stand out on crowded market shelves, where you are competing for the consumer's dollar with many other (usually less expensive) breads and other consumables. You want to make your breads appealing in every way so they are noticed and so your devoted customers can easily describe them to everyone they know.

WORDS TO KNOW

Gluten: A tough, elastic protein in flour.

Lecithin: A binder derived from soybeans that slows down the oxidation process and helps bread remain moist.

Quick breads: Breads that do not need yeast or kneading; the dough is mixed, put in a bread pan, and baked. Banana, cranberry, and nut breads are common quick breads.

RESOURCES

acitydiscount.com: suppliers of food service equipment

burford.com: commercial baking equipment

breadtopia.com: breadmaking instructional videos

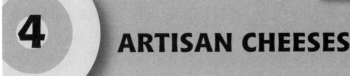

Artisan is the adjective currently in vogue that refers to handcrafted foodstuffs such as cheese, bread, and wine made in small batches (as opposed to mass produced). People appreciate the handcrafted aspect of these items and will pay accordingly. Not only do you provide high-quality food products, often made from locally grown ingredients, but you should also plan to package and present them in an artful way. Consumers will pay the higher price you need to put on these kinds of food items, but they want the entire product to be high quality, from taste to appearance to packaging to display to marketing.

Cheese is a perennially popular food and is remarkably easy to make. Cheese is, of course, made from dairy products, but it certainly doesn't have to be confined to cow's milk. Sheep's milk is also used for cheese, most notably for ricotta. One of the fastest-growing cheese items is goat cheese, which is a stronger-tasting, smooth cheese. Goats are smaller and easier to house and manage than cattle. They do, however, produce less milk, so the amount of cheese (called "chevre," which is French for "goat") you can make from one goat is considerably less than the amount you could make from one cow. That, combined with the fewer goat dairy herds compared to cow dairies, contributes to the higher price you can and need to command for goat cheese.

You can choose to purchase your milk from whatever type of dairy you wish. If you choose to start right from scratch, you can milk your own animals. "Farmstead cheese," according to the American Cheese Society, is by definition made from the milk produced by the cheesemaker's own flock of dairy animals. Building a flock of dairy animals with good milk production is a long but rewarding undertaking. In order to have milking cows, does, or ewes, they need to be bred and produce young. You need the land and buildings to do this—a big consideration especially with cattle. And you need to figure out what to do with the offspring; some females will go back into your milking herd, and the males are often sold as meat animals (see "farm-raised meat"). From there, you need to construct a dairy operation to milk the animals and store the milk in appropriately sanitary conditions.

Storage is an important issue, as cheeses are often aged. Northland Sheep Dairy, based in New York, ages their sheep-milk cheeses in a cheese cave anywhere from two months to two years, with the longer aging typically producing a sharper cheese.

THINGS TO CONSIDER

If you want to create your own cheese from your own milk source (known as "farmstead cheeses"), the animal husbandry will take a considerable amount of time. Milking needs to be done twice a day on a fairly rigid time schedule. If you want to make cheese but not deal with the animals, make arrangements to purchase milk from a local dairy. Or you can try to do it both ways, with a few animals of your own to create your farmstead cheeses and by purchasing the rest of the milk you need for an adequate amount of production.

HOW DO YOU WANT TO SPEND YOUR DAY?

Again, if you choose to raise your own animals to produce your own milk, you will need to spend a lot of your day dealing with the animals— feeding, milking, mucking barns, acquiring hay and feeds, tending to their health needs and medical problems, and so on. And then you need to make the cheese, although the cheesemaking itself is not terribly time consuming.

WHAT YOU WILL NEED

Home pasteurizers can be had for under $500, as can cream separators. You will also need a cheese press; the size you get will depend on the size mold you plan to use. Another big expense will be a refrigerator; size and style depends on how much cheese you plan to make. It doesn't have to be fancy, but it should be accurate in its refrigeration capabilities.

For small things, you will also need a dairy thermometer and a pH meter to test the acid level of the milk. And stainless steel will become your best friend, as you use everything from stainless steel pots to thermometers.

Finally, you will need cheesecloth for straining, draining, and wrapping (now you know where "cheesecloth" got its name!), cheese molds, waxes and wrappers for packaging, and knives and cheese slicers for prep or creating samples.

Of course, you will need a place to store all of this and to create your cheeses. In the beginning, you can do this in your own kitchen. But a refrigerator and storage for aging cheese will take more and more space as your business grows, so you need to consider if there is a place in your home to create more space, or if you will have to take your cheesemaking operation to another location. If you choose to run your own dairy, having a retail outlet may not be practical, unless you have a partner who will take on one or the other responsibility. But if you buy your milk from another source, you can more easily consider doing your cheesemaking at another site and even having a retail store.

MARKETING ANGLE

Farmer's markets, specialty shops that focus on local products, and high-end quality and "organic" supermarkets are the best outlets for your cheeses. You will need to decide whether to limit the market area or if you will sell to anyone who will buy your cheeses. If you package them attractively, most high-end markets will not be able to resist having your products in their store. And these markets often are not terribly price sensitive so you can price your cheeses as you need to.

NICE TOUCH

Plan to provide recipes or serving ideas with each cheese you sell. Customers need to be encouraged to buy, and the best way to do that is to give them tempting and easy ideas for how to use your products. Have a rack of different recipe cards; you can eventually plan to pull them all together into a book.

EXPANSION POSSIBILITIES

As with most businesses, it is better to start small. In the cheese business, it is good to start with a couple of specialties, perfect your technique, and get people talking about your products. Then you can begin to add other kinds of cheeses to your list. You could also begin to add meats if you raise your own animals. And if you are in the sheep dairy business or raise a couple of the goat breeds, there is the additional fiber element of fleeces and hair that can also be great products to sell.

Another great way to expand is to open a retail outlet. You can offer your cheeses as well as related products such as crackers, wine, cheese slicers, lovely dishware and serving pieces, and recipe books. And you can add some classes in home cheesemaking, how to use the cheeses that you sell, or what wines to serve with which cheeses.

WORDS TO KNOW

Cheese molds: Molds are used to make cheeses into certain shapes. Generally each type of cheese has a classic shape.

Trier: A tool that tests the readiness of cheeses without cutting them open. The trier is inserted into the center of the cheese and removes a sample core.

RESOURCES

artisancheesefestival.com: a California organization devoted to the promotion of and education about artisan cheesemaking

sheepdairying.com: The Sheep Dairy News

FOOD WRITER

5

Many ways exist to make money from writing about food. If you have a particular expertise, you could write a weekly column based on your food-related knowledge, such as quick meal ideas, grocery shopping tips, or even restaurant reviews. You could expand that idea into a monthly magazine column. And you can write books.

To become known as a food writer, plan to start small. Writers of any kind often run up against the old catch-22: You can't get published without clips (copies of your published articles) but you can't get clips without being published. Start by writing pieces for your local weekly newspaper, which you will probably have to do for free or for very little money. But these papers are often looking for editorial copy, so they are a good place for a beginner to get some experience. These articles are the beginnings of your clippings file.

Once you have a few pieces under your belt, you can begin to expand into the larger papers and magazines. If you are starting with absolutely no writing experience, you may want to take a class or two. This doesn't have to be an extensive undertaking—even a class through your area's community education program can help. What you need to understand at this point is what the differences are in writing for newspapers, writing for magazines, and writing books. Writing "feature" articles in newspapers is a bit like magazine writing, but is more concise and more tightly focused. Magazine articles have a little more room for details and allow you to be more thoughtful and opinionated (unless, of course, you are writing restaurant reviews for a newspaper, where opinion is mandatory!). Books are even more different still—publishers reject book ideas all the time because they is too topical and more suitable as a magazine article.

There are two main kinds of writers: those who are expert writers and those who are experts in something else and choose to pass their expertise along to others by writing about it. "Write what you know" is a good adage to adhere to at first. Start with the topic in which you have become expert, and write with authority.

Some topics are too narrow and will require you to expand your focus. For instance, if your expertise is cooking with sauces, at some point you will run out of writing material. You can work that angle longer by tackling it in different ways, such as writing about sauces that enhance flavor but aren't fattening, sauces you can freeze, and so on, but you can only write so many articles on this narrow topic. You will need to think about where you can go from there; for instance, adding marinades and other sauce-like recipes to your repertoire will take you beyond sauces into preparing the meats and dishes that one would use sauces.

THINGS TO CONSIDER

Depending on what approach you take, you can end up doing more writing work than food-related work. Only you can decide if that's OK—and you can have some control over that ratio. If you end up doing a lot of food writing projects, you will inevitably end up in front of a computer screen a lot. Doing recipe books can be fun, but you will need to gain access to a test kitchen, you may need to hire a couple of testers to help you, and you need to buy ingredients—some publishers may provide a budget for that in your contract, but probably not unless you know to ask!

HOW DO YOU WANT TO SPEND YOUR DAY?

Being the kind of writer who is an expert in something and writes about it is a bit of the best of both worlds syndrome: you get to do what you really enjoy and then sit down and work at a computer. In the case of food work, the "doing" is active and interactive. You are most likely on your feet and moving around the kitchen while you are working with food, you will need to go grocery shopping, or you are dining out as a food critic or shopping around for the best place to buy prepared baba ganoush. The other part of your time is spent sitting in an office chair, staring at the computer screen, and working on a keyboard. Just when you feel like you would like to sit down or would like to get up, it's time to do just that!

WHAT YOU WILL NEED

You will need the components of whatever food expertise you bring to the table—that is up to you. You will need to have a decent computer with a comfortable workstation as well as a printer and the other basic peripherals. You will also need a phone and fax machine to facilitate communications with publications.

MARKETING ANGLE

Marketing oneself as a writer with expertise in a particular subject is a bit less complicated than marketing oneself as a professional writer. The markets you will reach out to are more focused, which makes them also fewer in number, but, in general, the food-related market is pretty big. Be sure to focus on your particular expertise. Explain why it is important and why people (and in particular, that publication's readership) will want to read what you write. Consider creating a simple brochure about your food-related experience. List on the brochure any published credentials you have, the more recent the better. You can create this brochure in a basic program such as Microsoft Publisher, which comes with Microsoft's Office Suites software. Decent printers can be bought for short money these days, which will allow you to print a dozen or so brochures at a time. Because this isn't the kind of brochure you will stack up at the dentist's office, you only need a few to send to prospective publishing outlets and you only need to print up a few at a time.

NICE TOUCH

You can expand your marketability as a food writer if you become adept with a digital camera. Although professional food photography is an art form, you can at the very least accompany your newspaper articles with photos. Not all articles have to be about food itself—perhaps you are doing a series of profiles about local chefs or restaurant entrepreneurs. Taking your own pictures can be a big boost.

EXPANSION POSSIBILITIES

A natural expansion is the one mentioned above, of progressing from newspaper writing—which can go from free to cheap to real money when you can get a weekly column or even modestly syndicated—to magazine writing, which pays more per article, to book writing which pays in royalties. Financially, book writing can be "the sky's the limit," but don't count on it—those books that unexpectedly take off are few and far between.

Another way you can expand is to team up with someone. Food writers have teamed up with well-known companies to create recipes that use the company's products. Consumers like these books—they offer shortcuts and interesting options for creating quick, interesting meals.

WORDS TO KNOW

Column inches: A measurement used by newspapers to determine how long a piece will be.

Syndication: A regular column—often weekly, when it is in a newspaper—that is carried by many different newspapers around the country. This is usually done through a syndication service that sells the idea to newspapers nationwide.

Word count: A measurement typically used by magazines and book publishers to define how long a piece will be.

RESOURCES

cookspalate.com

writers-publish.com

6 COOKING CLASSES

Teaching about food and cooking to others can take on many different forms. You could start a consulting business where you

- go into people's homes and help them set up more effective and efficient kitchens
- teach them how to stock their pantries to have ingredients on hand that would allow them to put together a meal on a moment's notice
- help them pick out the most appropriate and useful cookware and utensils for their lifestyle and cooking needs
- teach them how to shop for herbs, spices, basics such as rice and pasta, and fresh produce
- actually teach them how to cook specific dishes, follow recipes, and make dishes to freeze.

Or you could take a more traditional route and teach cooking classes. This could take on many forms as well, such as teaching how to

- cook for children
- cook with certain ingredients, such as wine, sauces, or seafood
- make ethnic foods, from antipasto to sushi to empanadas to pad thai
- create inexpensive dishes from simple ingredients

- make dishes that can be frozen

- can and freeze fruits and vegetables

- prepare meals on the grill

- create low-fat and special diet meals.

This list is literally endless. You decide in which area you are qualified to teach and go from there. People are always looking for ways to save money or time while still eating and feeding their families healthful and satisfying meals.

Once you determine what you might like to teach, you need to find a venue. There are several options:

- Consider doing a round robin-type class, where each week (or month, or however frequently you decide to hold your class) you travel to a different member of the class's home and teach there. This is something you would have to make clear up front; if one student doesn't have an appropriate setup, you can either do it more than once at another site, or you can do it your house.

- Rent a commercial kitchen that is set up for classes.

- Create an appropriate space in your own home. Renovating your kitchen is well beyond the $5,000 limitations of this book, but if you really look at your current kitchen, you could most likely figure out how to make it work. Just keep your class sizes to an appropriate number.

THINGS TO CONSIDER

You will be working with the public, and your clients will have great expectations from you. It will be important to keep it fun.

HOW DO YOU WANT TO SPEND YOUR DAY?

Cooking classes means being on your feet a lot. Not only will you be standing in front of the counter, stove, oven, and so on, but you will be shopping for the ingredients you need at the local grocery store.

WHAT YOU WILL NEED

You will need an oven, stove, counters, and chairs for students; although they can stand around the counter to watch, eventually you will want chairs for them. You will also need all the cooking paraphernalia of pot holders, utensils, napkins, towels, paper towels, and every possible cooking utensil.

MARKETING ANGLE

The best way to market yourself as a cooking teacher is to come up with a specialty. You can always expand on that specialty later, but you need a hook to hang your hat on. Just offering "cooking classes" is not going to attract anyone. They want to know what you are teaching and whether it is something they would like to learn how to cook or to cook better than they do already.

NICE TOUCH

Make sure to have some take-home materials, such as a print out of the recipe for that class, including a photo of the finished recipe. This makes people feel they got more for their money, and it is good publicity when a student leaves the brochure or recipe hanging around the house and others see it.

EXPANSION POSSIBILITIES

One simple way to expand when it comes to teaching is to take on more students. Once you are teaching one student, it often doesn't matter if you are teaching seven more or 20 more. You can keep things manageable by having people work in teams. Classes are often just a socializing time for many people; partnering gives them an automatic reason to do just that.

WORDS TO KNOW

Knife skills: The proper choice of knife and knowing how to use different knives; also includes sharpening techniques and how to choose the best cutting surfaces.

Nouvelle cuisine: A type of cuisine that focuses on light dishes, avoids heavy sauces, and uses fresh seasonal produce.

RESOURCES

ehow.com/how_2054510_teach-cooking-class.html

localcookingclass.com

mymommybiz.com/ideas/cookingclass.html

7 MAPLE SYRUP PRODUCTION/SALES

You have to be in the right area of the country or in Canada to produce maple syrup, but if you are, the rewards are more than just the sweet brown liquid: Maple syrup currently sells for over $40 a gallon.

The first thing you need to make syrup is sap from the sugar maple tree (*Acer saccharum*). The sugar maple range is predominantly in the northeastern part of North America. In the spring, when northern days turn warmer but nights are still cold, the sap of the maple tree begins to "run." The trees are tapped, and the sap is collected. The clear, watery liquid is then boiled down to the point of a thick, sweet liquid and bottled to sell to people to put on their pancakes, oatmeal, and ice cream.

Having a stand of maple trees is a process of its own. You can buy a property with an existing stand. Many old country farms have maple trees that line the driveway. Or you can plant saplings for your future maple syrup production plans. However, as relatively slow growers, your saplings will take 10 to 15 years to reach a trunk diameter large enough to tap for sap, so you will be planning long-term if you take this route.

Another way to get sap without having trees yourself is to find someone who owns a sugar maple stand who doesn't tap their trees and ask if you can tap them yourself. You can "rent" the trees from them, although most likely you can exchange the use of their trees for some of the syrup production. If you do go this route, be sure to take very good care of the trees, collect the sap daily, keep the tapping sites tidy, and clear out your equipment after the season (which lasts anywhere from three to eight weeks) is over.

The boiling process can be as simple as putting a pot full of sap on the stove and letting it simmer. Be prepared to have a room full of steam for hours; if you have wallpaper in your kitchen or nearby rooms, you may not want to go this route! People also boil sap on their woodstoves or on a gas-fired stovetop outside. However, if you want to do anything commercially with maple syrup, you need to get more efficient than that.

Maple syrup "evaporators" are available in several different sizes; choose one according to your access to trees and sap and how much time and effort you intend to put into the production of syrup. If you have a full-time job, you can still do maple production, but to do it on a commercial scale, you will need to get up a couple hours earlier than usual to collect your sap collection and spend at least every other evening boiling, again depending on how much sap you collect.

An evaporator is essentially a big woodstove with a stainless steel pan that fits tightly on top and is specially designed for boiling sap. As the sap thickens, it moves along in partitions, pushing the thicker sap toward the final partition, where it can be drawn off through a valve in the side of the pan.

Start relatively small with your evaporator. You will need to build a small building (a sap house) to house your evaporator; it does not need to be anything elaborate and can be easily built for less than $5,000. You can even start out in the open or under a small canopy, but it won't be as pleasant for you!

Once you become proficient at making the syrup, think about upgrading to a bigger evaporator. This actually can become less time consuming. Even though you produce more syrup, the bigger evaporator can handle more sap at a time.

The larger evaporators are also equipped with warming pans into which you pour the cold sap, so it is preheated before you allow it to join the sap in the partitioned pan. These small features can considerably reduce the time it takes to boil the sap down to syrup.

It takes 40 gallons of sap to make just one gallon of syrup, so you can see why maple syrup is referred to as liquid gold.

THINGS TO CONSIDER

Maple syrup production is not for the faint of heart. You need to be able to lift heavy buckets of sap, stand on your feet for long hours to monitor the boiling sap as it becomes syrup, and carry, cut, and stack firewood. However, with a little ingenuity, all of these things can be made less physically tasking. You could, for example, mount the collection tank in a truck, on a trailer behind a snowmobile, or even hire local teenage football players to carry the buckets of sap for you. You could install a gas-fired evaporator instead of a wood-fired one and sit on a tall stool near the evaporator. It's all doable. The one thing you can't change is that you will need to be outside a lot, so that should be something you enjoy. Another thing to keep in mind is the seasonality of the maple syrup business. You could be boiling for just three weeks or as many as eight, but once the nights get warmer, the sap stops running and you are out of business until next year.

HOW DO YOU WANT TO SPEND YOUR DAY?

Again, you need to like being outside. But no matter what part of the maple syrup business you don't like, the season is over in a relatively short time.

WHAT YOU WILL NEED

Your two biggest expenses will be an evaporator, which costs anywhere from $750 to $2000, and something to give it and you shelter. Evaporators can be bought used, because people regularly go in and out of this business. You also should plan to get some sort of shed or shelter; it should something as simple as a canopy or perhaps a prefab shed, but remember that if you start with a small evaporator and your business expansion plans include a bigger evaporator, you will eventually need more room. So be sure your shed can be expanded if necessary.

You'll also need containers for collecting the sap. The old-fashioned route uses metal buckets that are wider at the top than the bottom and have lids that slide on the edge. These hook onto metal hooks that are attached to the "spiles" that you pound into the tree. More modern methods include small plastic spiles to which tubing is attached and connected to several other trees, all of which collect into a single collection tank. This method is much less attractive but much more efficient.

You will need a supply of wood to fire your evaporator—or gas, if you go that route. You will probably want a finishing pan, which is typically a small gas unit with a stainless steel pan where you can bring the sap to its final thickness and filter the syrup as you run it off. You will need filters and a candy thermometer to determine when the sap is syrup. And you will need a selection of bottles to put the final product in.

If you plan to sell your syrup at a farmer's market or elsewhere, you will need labels and tags with your business name and the price.

MARKETING ANGLE

Maple syrup markets itself, but there are a lot of syrup producers so you need to find someone who would like a local product in their store. You can also sell via the internet with a website of your own. Create a unique name—but keep in mind that any of the generic-sounding maple syrup names have long been taken!

NICE TOUCH

Everyone knows you pour maple syrup on your pancakes, but syrup is good for a lot more than that. Give a small brochure of recipes with each syrup purchase and encourage customers to use your syrup for many things—they will need more a lot faster that way!

EXPANSION POSSIBILITIES

Expansion in this business is limited to your ability to get sap. And no matter how hard you try to squeeze sap out of a sugar maple, once the sap stops running, the season is over. What you will need to do is find some business ideas for the off season, which could include teaching some cooking classes that utilize maple syrup in the recipes you create.

WORDS TO KNOW

Spiles: The piece of metal or plastic that is tapped into the tree through which the sap runs.

Tubing: A series of taps connected by plastic tubing, all of which run to a large container that collects the sap from several trees/taps.

RESOURCES

fullerssugarhouse.com

maplesyrupsupplies.com

PICNIC BASKETS

8

This romantic business could be done as an on-demand service like any gift basket service. The simplest way to start would be to appeal to couples to create special picnic baskets for a walk in the park or a day at the beach.

In this era of weight-watching and health consciousness, consider having a healthy selection of picnic baskets. Other ideas would be to have a "locally made" basket that includes items made with local produce, meats, and from local bakeries and beverage companies.

You could add ethnic selections if you keep it simple: you don't want to have thousands of products on hand that may be chosen once a month. But if there is an Asian market nearby or a Chinese chef who might make you some individual-sized noodle salads, you could have a unique offering.

You will need a storefront to do a picnic basket service. You could try to team up with an existing market such as a local country store, to sell your baskets. If they can accommodate you in the building and give you a small corner, that would be ideal. Perhaps the local convenience store has a deli section that already makes sandwiches, and you could purchase the sandwiches from them at a wholesale price and pay for them up at the end of each day. There are numerous ways this arrangement can be arranged, so think creatively!

To keep the price affordable, you could rent the picnic baskets to customers with a deposit for the full price in case one is not returned. Use a specific kind of basket or stamp them with your business name and offer a discount on the next picnic to anyone who returns the basket. A picnic basket itself as a gift—without the comestibles—would be another great option to add to your offerings. Include nice plasticware utensils, plates, cups, napkins, a picnic tablecloth, and salt-and-pepper shakers and market your baskets as great shower, wedding, and anniversary gifts. Be sure to include a discount coupon for the gift-recipient to have the basket filled for their picnics!

If you are in northern climates, you will want to promote some winter picnic ideas. Create a basket for snowmobilers, cross-country skiers, and snowshoers. There is no reason why they can't return to the car after their ski through the woods and enjoy a tailgate picnic. Or, create a "backpack picnic" that can be enjoyed trailside.

THINGS TO CONSIDER

This business includes working with perishables. Learn to order with precision and think of things to offer that have a long shelf life.

Decide whether you want to have an a la carte menu, or you want to offer a regular menu of picnic options where the picnickers perhaps choose only their sandwich selection.

HOW DO YOU WANT TO SPEND YOUR DAY?

You will be dealing with the public regularly in this business, so you need to enjoy providing customer service. People are incredibly fussy about their food, so you need to understand how to develop menus and create something that people will love.

WHAT YOU WILL NEED

You will need picnic baskets, but keep it simple and choose no more than two or three different kinds of baskets. You will need the paraphernalia that goes in the baskets, from the napkins and utensils to the food itself. Be conservative in your food purchasing at first; as a startup, you want to be sure you know what sells best before filling a refrigerator with it.

You will also need a refrigerator, probably a separate freezer, a microwave, and a cash register. You will need to accept credit cards of several kinds. And you will need some display space for sample baskets.

MARKETING ANGLE

Word-of-mouth is going to be very important for this business. You are selling an experience, not just food, and you want people to talk about it so their friends, acquaintances, business associates, and others will all want to come to you for that great experience.

Word of mouth is important, but for this business to succeed, you will need to do some marketing. People need to know you exist. Create a simple brochure and place copies everywhere and anywhere you can. Start a mailing list, an e-mail list, and a website, and get the word out.

You will need to constantly remind people how much fun their picnic was and encourage them to do it again. Set up a couple mock picnics and, if you have a high-quality digital camera, take pictures. Having a professional take pictures for you can get expensive, but showing a couple enjoying a picnic they bought from you can be enticing.

NICE TOUCH

Don't forget that people often take their dogs when they spend time outdoors. Include dog biscuits and small water containers for the pooch's picnic and dog lovers will love your baskets!

Another special touch could be to offer a "proposal picnic basket" where a picnic basket can provide a way to hide the ring or a proposal note—perhaps even in a fortune cookie!

EXPANSION POSSIBILITIES

Assuming you start small, you can branch out by adding different kinds of picnics; perhaps including large-scale events in your offerings. Expanding your menu is always a way to expand your business, as in offering both lower- and higher-priced picnics. And if working out of a retail location works well, you could open a sandwich shop with a small seating area to help keep the perishables moving.

WORDS TO KNOW

Picnic: From the French term "pique-nique," meaning a fashionable social entertainment in which each party present contributes a share of the provisions.
Wine duffels: Cloth bags designed to hold a bottle of wine.

RESOURCES

basket4picnic.com: picnicking lore and recipes for picnic foods.
picnicsupplyworld.com
webstaurantstore.com: suppliers of quality plasticware

Mmm-mm, everyone loves barbecue! Secret recipes abound for the best barbecue sauce, from sweet to spicy. If you like making barbecue, start experimenting with your own sauce and then market it. With a sauce that is unique and delicious enough, you could sell just the sauce. Bottle it, create a fun label and a website, and sell your BBQ sauce yourself. You can market it to stores that are interested in locally made products, or you can go the distance and also sell meat marinated with your sauce.

Selling barbecued meat can be done in several ways. You can set up a chuck wagon and take it to gatherings, offer it as a catering opportunity at events and functions, or bring it to fairs and festivals. People appreciate good food at these kinds of events. Add some corn bread, corn-on-the-cob, cole slaw, or other sides and a dessert, and voila! You have a chuck wagon worth remembering.

THINGS TO CONSIDER

To do this kind of thing for fairs and festivals, you need to learn how to cook for large numbers of people. Barbecue is perfect for cooking for a crowd. You will need to learn how to shop in large quantities for all the ingredients you need, from onions to spices to tomato paste.

HOW DO YOU WANT TO SPEND YOUR DAY?

To create the sauce, you will be on your feet a lot standing in front of the stove, although simmering barbecue doesn't need to be watched constantly. This is an indoor job, but you can probably do a lot of your cooking at night. If you are operating the chuck wagon, you'll be on your feet as well, but outdoors instead.

WHAT YOU WILL NEED

You will need large pots for simmering your barbecue, either just the sauce or the marinating meat. You will need a heat source—what kind depends on how you plan to sell your barbecue. A chuck wagon for the fair may be beyond the $5,000 scope of this book, although you may be able to lease a booth at the fair.

If you are making sauce and selling it, you will need bottles. Create labels for the bottles that are fun and memorable.

MARKETING ANGLE

Barbecue is often thought of as a summer thing, so to keep your product selling year-round, you need to market the message that barbecue is a perfect winter comfort food.

NICE TOUCH

Offer free samples to people who are considering whether to buy your barbecue or move on to the Italian sausage booth. And if you are selling bottled sauce, don't leave potential customers to wonder what they would do with a whole jar of sauce once they have it at home; provide them with a few simple, mouth-watering recipes for how they can use your sauce in their own kitchens. Post these recipes so customers can read and discuss them, and not have to just take your word for it that your sauces have a lot of uses and are a great take-home item. Plenty of people like to have a variety of sauces at home, and specialty bottled sauces make a great gifts for those folks as well.

EXPANSION POSSIBILITIES

Once you have a good recipe that is selling, expansion is limitless in terms of adding retailers to reach a wider market. If you go the BBQ chuck wagon route, you can add wagons and hire people to work for you so you can cover multiple events on the same day. As long as it is your sauce, the product will be the same.

WORDS TO KNOW

Mesquite: A southwestern shrub that bears pods that are rich in sugar and, when used for grilling, provide a rich smoky flavor.

Brisket: cut of meat from the breast area of the animal

Rubs: dry spices that are rubbed on meat before cooking

RESOURCES

bbqadvisor.com

bbqgalore.com

10 HOT DOG CART

Despite the questionable ingredients in some hot dogs, it is hard to imagine these treats ever going out of style. They are the perfect hand food, they are filling, and with condiments for each individual taste, they are delicious.

Enter the hot dog cart. Perhaps you live near a small town where you could set your cart up on the town square and sell hot dogs at lunch time.

Hot dogs are perennial bestselling lunch items. But you don't have to rely on the same old cheap "mystery meat" kind of hot dogs. Purchase high-quality hot dogs and charge the appropriate price for them. You can also get chicken dogs, turkey dogs, and other hot-dog-like spin-offs that have become popular with more health-conscious consumers.

THINGS TO CONSIDER

You will be working with the public, which is something you need to enjoy in order to be successful at this kind of operation. You could become known as the curmudgeonly hot dog salesperson in the middle of town, but that probably isn't the best approach to take. Your reputation should be based on having the best hot dog in a 30-mile radius, but you also want to be friendly and have people enjoy being your customer. Keep up on the local news and engage people in conversation. Friendliness means people will like you, which makes them think of you as their friend, and this keeps them coming back as loyal customers.

You will be on your feet when your hot dog cart is open, but the duration of the lunch business period isn't terrifically long.

HOW DO YOU WANT TO SPEND YOUR DAY?

Your hot dog day could look something like this:

9:30 a.m.:   Stock your vehicle with any bulk inventory such as buns, dogs, etc.

10:30 a.m.:   Get to your stand and begin to open: Get the hot dog steamer going, the condiment holders filled, the napkin supply in place.

11:30 a.m.:   Open up and sell some dogs!

2:00 p.m.:   Clean and close your stand. Go to the bank and deposit the day's receipts.

You can stay open a little longer, if you can catch an afternoon crowd. At least one day a week, you need to do your bookkeeping and order supplies.

WHAT YOU WILL NEED

You will need a cart or stand. To stick within your $5,000 limit, you will need to either lease or build a cart. You will need a hot dog steamer, but start modestly. You can always trade up if your business takes off and your steamer doesn't hold enough dogs. Get a couple of sets of tongs to lift the steaming dogs and buns out of the steamer. You will want stainless steel containers for relish and onions and serving spoons. Ketchup and mustard—and get a few different kinds of mustard, as people like a choice—can be left in their squeeze containers.

Besides hot dogs, you should plan to sell chips and drinks. The chip distributor should be able to supply you with a chip stand to suit your setup. You'll need some sort of refrigeration for drinks. A cooler might do the job, depending on how much business you do. And remember, you are likely going to be outside with this venture, so everything needs to be secured on windy days!

And finally, in most places, you need a license to run a vending cart. Make sure to check what permits your town or city requires before setting up shop, and find out what limitations there may be on where you can locate your cart or stand.

MARKETING ANGLE

You don't need to do much traditional marketing for a hot dog stand. People who work near town or happen to be around at lunchtime will be your customers. It is unlikely that people from other towns would come to your town just to eat at your hot dog stand—at least not at first! If your dogs are exceptional, and you find a way to be unique, word of mouth will be the best advertising you can get. And don't underestimate the effect of an enticing aroma of hot dogs on hungry passersby!

NICE TOUCH

A nice touch for any business is to offer a frequent-customer coupon. This could be "buy ten dogs and the eleventh one is free" or offer a considerable discount if they hand you a card with ten punches in it. Punching cards can be a bit of a pain during the busy lunch rush, but be prepared with a hole punch on a string right near the cash register where you won't lose it.

EXPANSION POSSIBILITIES

You can always expand your offerings to other types of dogs such as chili dogs or hot dogs and sauerkraut. Or you can go beyond hot dogs to other sandwiches or perhaps add cookies or side dishes such as coleslaw. But don't dilute your hot dog operation too much. In this type of business, it is more profitable to be the best at one thing than to spread yourself too thin.

WORDS TO KNOW

Revocation: When a license is taken away or revoked for infractions of any rules imposed on vendors by the state or city in which they operate.

Counter-style cart: A cart that includes a service counter for customers; the counter can simply be a place to set hot dogs while the customer pays or adds condiments, or it can provide a space for customers to eat either standing or sitting on stools.

Fleet: Having more than one hot dog cart in various locations.

RESOURCES

streetvendor.netfirms.com: The Street Vendor Project website contains news, articles, and blogs about New York City street vending, but it is interesting for anyone considering this business.

11 MEALS-TO-GO

E veryone seems to get busier and busier. Who wouldn't appreciate a service that provides them with healthy, delicious meals they don't have to cook themselves? You can do that with a meals-to-go business.

Start by picking a couple of dishes that you feel comfortable making in quantity. Pick a night of the week to offer meals to go. Friday tends to be a night when people go out to eat, the weekend is more leisurely, and Monday and Tuesday people still tend to be fresh and optimistic about their ability to prepare an evening meal. But you could help people get over the hump on Wednesday by providing a good meal for them to pick up on the way home. Thursday seems to be the evening of exhaustion before the final push on Friday, which makes Thursday another good possibility for a meal-to-go night.

Once you have a couple of good ideas for meals and you've picked a night, you need to start to convince people to consider your option. Post signs to let potential customers know that help is on the way.

You will definitely want a website. This is a great way for your customers to learn about your business and to look up what you will be serving in a given week so they can make their plans. Put your web address on everything—your sign, your brochures, and your business cards. Encourage website visitors to sign up in advance and pay through credit card or PayPal so you can have a better sense of how many customers you will be feeding each week. Encourage them to fill out short online surveys to learn more about what people would like you to serve.

To get some startup capital, consider offering a discount for advance payment for multiple weeks.

Don't get stuck in a bland casserole rut. Although you need to make things that are good candidates for making in large quantities and that will freeze well, you also want to use the very highest quality ingredients and keep vegetarian and health concerns in mind. Be creative with flavors, colors, and textures, and don't forget the salads and desserts!

This is a business that will take time to reach critical mass. Don't get discouraged; plan small and grow big. An important decision is to find a way for your customers to easily pick up their food. Your home would have to have a very specific setup (and possibly commercial zoning) to make it appropriate for customers to drive in and pick up their meals. You want a lot of business, but you don't want cars lined up in your driveway trying not to hit each other. People would also prefer not to have to get out of their cars to collect their meals. Look for an old drive-through or big parking lot where you could set up out of a wagon or some other easy way for customers to collect their dinners.

THINGS TO CONSIDER

You won't have the same number of customers each week. Don't get discouraged by the fact that some weeks you have a lot of leftover food. It takes time to learn how to plan your food purchases and to develop a steady clientele.

HOW DO YOU WANT TO SPEND YOUR DAY?

In this business, you will spend your day cooking—or at least your afternoon. Then you need to be around in the late afternoon/early evening for people to pick up their food as they make their way home from work.

WHAT YOU WILL NEED

You will need to be able to cook significant quantities of food and keep entrees hot until the customers pick them up. This means you need a reliable commercial oven, and maybe more than one. You don't have to buy a new one; you may be able to find used equipment or find a facility where you can lease space.

You will need to purchase the appropriate serving items for the kinds of food you plan to make.

Although packaging is a concern for any food-related business, in the meals-to-go business in particular you really need to have appropriate packaging, especially if your customer may not be at home when you deliver.

MARKETING ANGLE

Appealing to the busy family is certainly the key marketing angle here. Healthy meals made from quality ingredients that are ready to eat—all you have to do is enjoy your family's company!

NICE TOUCH

Donate leftover food to homeless shelters and halfway houses. These nonprofit services are always looking for donations. Make sure it is decently packaged and has been stored appropriately. Many places will come to your location to pick up any unsold food.

EXPANSION POSSIBILITIES

Your quickest expansion will be adding another day of the week to your service. Otherwise, just keep adding customers! If your food is good, and you are reliable, the idea will catch on.

WORDS TO KNOW

Comfort food: This term has come to refer to foods that make people feel good, perhaps reminding them of their childhood. Macaroni-and-cheese, lasagna, mashed potatoes are all thought of as "comfort foods."

Packaging: Meals-to-go will require specific packaging, depending on the meal being offered. The packaging may need compartments to ensure that one item doesn't spill into another, or it may need to keep a meal hot or cold.

RESOURCES

angelfire.com: a website with recipes for crowds

dinewise.com: an example of a prepared meals business

dinnersdone.net: a self-serve variation on the prepared meals business

ellenskitchen.com: another website with large-size recipes

12 GOURMET POPCORN

Popcorn is a long-standing favorite treat. Gourmet popcorn, especially in exotic flavors, takes snacking on popcorn to a new level. A popcorn business is relatively uncomplicated and can be approached in several ways.

Fairs and other events are a great place to sell popcorn. You can keep it simple with a popcorn popper on wheels that makes basic popcorn, and then you can add the customer's choice of flavors. Besides the popper, all you need are two or three different container sizes, an assortment of flavorings, and napkins, and you have your popcorn business!

If you decide you want to do more with your popcorn business, you can skip the fairs and festivals, create larger volumes of flavored popcorn, and sell it via a website to people all over the country or the world. You will need a larger volume popper, sealable containers of varying sizes and types, and packaging for shipping the containers of popcorn. You'll also need to create a website that is fun and (excuse the expression) pops!

Another approach you can take is to sell to the major gift-food businesses such Harry & David. The bigger companies will already have regular gourmet popcorn suppliers, but perhaps you can become the popcorn supplier to the next level of gift food businesses. The Harry & Davids of the world will come knocking at your door when they discover that your popcorn is selling phenomenally well.

THINGS TO CONSIDER

Unless you can afford to buy an enormous-size popper, you will spend a lot of your day (or night) on your feet making popcorn. Of course, if your business plan can accommodate it, you can hire someone to do this aspect of the business for you, both at home and fairs, while you concentrate on things such as marketing and finding large wholesales customers.

HOW DO YOU WANT TO SPEND YOUR DAY?

As long as you keep close tabs on quality control and don't let employee costs get out of hand, you can farm out the parts of the business you either don't enjoy or are not a good use of your time. It is always important to start a business doing every aspect that keeps the business functioning yourself. That way, you know how everything is done, can understand employee concerns, and can appreciate how hard it is to do certain things well. And you can always step in to perform any job in your business if someone is sick or quits.

WHAT YOU WILL NEED

You will, of course, need something with which to pop corn. And you will need the corn to pop. Machines to use at fairs and other stands can cost as much as $1,500. The largest ones are over $3,000, but a 32-ounce capacity compared to 18 ounces for half the price or less is not very cost effective.

Containers come as cones, bags—both plastic and paper—and boxes. The kernels run around $13 for a gallon container. You will also need popping oil and salt. You can choose to use flavored butter or seasoned salt, but to make true gourmet popped corn, you will want to create your own special seasonings. You can always use the old standbys—caramel corn, kettle corn, and cheddar-flavored popcorn—but add your own gourmet flavors to appeal to more customers.

If you decide to go into the wholesale or retail popcorn business, you will need to search for just the right container in which to sell your popcorn. Your packaging can make your products stand out from the crowd.

MARKETING ANGLE

You aren't marketing popcorn specifically, but competing in the huge arena of snack foods and food gifts. Appeal to that aspect in all your marketing materials, from print flyers and advertisements to your website. Look at other snack food gift businesses and see how they go about appealing to people.

NICE TOUCH

Brainstorm some ways to make your gourmet popcorn special. You could mimic Cracker Jacks and hide a message in the popcorn container. You could have messages or game prizes stuck to the underside of a can of popcorn. A popcorn bag could include a crossword puzzle. Or the messages you offer could be personalized, so people could send a message to a popcorn gift recipient.

Another nice touch is to include a hand wipe with your container of popcorn.

EXPANSION POSSIBILITIES

There are many ways to expand from popcorn. The natural ones would be the types of snacks you would find at fairs, such as cotton candy, roasted almonds, and peanuts of many different types.

WORDS TO KNOW

Agitator blade: A propeller-like device that spreads the popcorn around the cabinet (the term used for the container in which the corn is popped).

Warming deck: A heating element that keeps the bottom tray of the popcorn machine warm, which keeps the popped corn warm and fresh.

RESOURCES

popcornsupply.com

popsezpopcorn.com

13 HERB SALES

$

Locally grown products are the wave of the future. People now want to buy food that is grown closer to home and requires less use of fossil fuels for transport. They also want more information about how their food is grown, such as what kinds of chemical fertilizers and pesticides are used.

Herbs are beautiful, useful, and easy to grow. They don't take up a lot of space, and most can do well with a minimum amount of care. If you have a sizeable patch of land that is available and appropriate for gardens, growing herbs can be approached in a few different ways.

Your patch of land doesn't need to be enormous to grow herbs. Of course, the more you can grow, the more you can sell, and the more money you can make. But a lot depends on what you do with the final product.

You will need to decide whether you will sell your herbs live, picked and packed, or dried. To sell live plants, it is best to plant them in the pots in which you will sell them, rather than putting them through the shock of transplantation twice—once from your garden to the pot, and then from the pot to the purchaser's garden.

If you plan to market to cooks and not gardeners, you will probably want to sell your herbs either fresh-picked and packed in sealed bags or picked, dried, and sold in baggies. You can also consider a "pick-your-own" arrangement, which is popular these days and saves you work; however, herbs are more delicate than most PYO products like pears, apples, or berries. You may save your garden a lot of strife and your plants a lot of wear and tear if you do the picking.

Be sure to display the herbs you are selling in an attractive stand or shed. Clean the pots, make sure to pull out weeds and straggling grass, and water them well. Create tags with transplanting and care instructions so the herb's new owner can be successful with their new acquisition.

If you are selling dried or fresh cut herbs for culinary use, include some ideas for use or short recipes in order to entice people to buy the herbs and be able to use them without having to research a recipe themselves. This can create more impulse purchases, as opposed to the people who come to your herb stand with a particular herb in mind.

HOW THIS BUSINESS IMPACTS YOUR HOME

Depending on the size of your property, you may end up using substantial outdoor space for your herb garden. As mentioned above, you can sell your herbs in a farmstand, the nursery down the road, or the farmer's market in the bank parking lot on Saturday morning—it's up to you (and your local zoning laws) whether you have customers coming to your home or not.

THINGS TO CONSIDER

In the northern parts of the country, this is going to be a seasonal endeavor. Even if you decide to grow your herbs in the summer and then spend the winter making dried arrangements, etc., you will still only be making money on your products during part of the year.

If you choose to sell your herbs to a nursery who will in turn sell them to their customers, you need to be prepared to discount them up to 50 percent of what you would charge if you sold them directly to the customer yourself. This can work if you have a large amount of herbs to sell.

HOW DO YOU WANT TO SPEND YOUR DAY?

You will want to enjoy being outdoors and perhaps even swatting a few flies in order to be a gardener. You can't mind getting your hands and clothes dirty. Some of the time, you will need to either deal with customers who come to your garden or booth at the farmer's market to purchase their plants or with vendors where you sell your herbs.

WHAT YOU WILL NEED

You will need a patch of land that will hold the size garden you want—or barring that, you can often rent a garden space in a community plot, although you may find you will soon outgrow that space.

If you don't already have a green thumb, consider taking a class or two to help you ensure your planting success.

You will need gardening tools, and do yourself a favor and get buy good quality tools with ergonomic handles. If you love gardening, you already know the joy of having proper tools.

To prepare your garden, you may need to bring in a load of loam. Consider raised beds, which are neat looking and easier to manage. And you will need seeds of the various herbs you plan to grow.

Depending on the size of your business and whether you set up to sell from your home or take your herbs elsewhere, you may want a small pickup truck to transport your plants.

If you choose to sell plants, you will need plant containers as well as tags that identify and describe care and transplanting instructions. If you decide to sell fresh clipped herbs, you will need a refrigerator, plastic bags, and adhesive labels that you can use with your computer to print out the name of the herb.

MARKETING ANGLE

Once you decide whether you are going to sell mostly fresh plants to gardeners (who may or may not be chefs) or fresh picked or dried herbs to chefs, then you can create targeted marketing materials. If you decide to sell to the gardener market, post notices for your herbs in places such as restaurant bulletin boards or hardware stores. If you are selling to chefs, investigate whether there is a cook's newsletter in the area or perhaps if someone offers cooking classes. You could also target area high-quality restaurants; they generally love to advertise that their meals are prepared with local, fresh herbs.

NICE TOUCH

Any agricultural venture can enhance their image by going organic. Although it takes a long time and often a lot of expense to be certified organic, you can promote the fact that you use natural pest-deterring measures, no pesticides, and only organic fertilizers to grow your herbs. This will matter a lot if you sell your herbs to people who plan to cook with them.

If you decide to sell clipped herbs specifically for cooking, consider adding a recipe or two to each package. Also, you can sell herbed vinegars and oils as well as the fresh herbs themselves. Better yet, sell the herbs in a container with instructions on how buyers can make their own herbed oils and vinegars.

EXPANSION POSSIBILITIES

You could start as small as you like and sell herbs from a picnic table with an honor box outside your home. From there, you could expand to selling at farmer's markets. You could then begin to market to restaurants and keep yourself busy most of the growing season supplying those two venues. If you have the space, you could expand your selling season by drying herbs in the fall and making herbal-flavored oils and vinegars to sell as gifts for the holidays, again either on the roadside or through a local retail outlet that might be willing to carry your products or perhaps to a gift basket business that might be interested in designing a basket around your bottled herbal vinegars and oils.

WORDS TO KNOW

Ag-Tourism: "agricultural tourism;" agricultural businesses that have created a destination for tourists with things such as hay rides, farmstands, maple syrup production, and so on.

Culinary: Of or for cooking; when herbs are used for flavoring food, it is referred to as "culinary usage."

PYO: "Pick your own." At a PYO farm, the customers pick their own fruit or vegetables right out of the orchard or garden. Also known as "you pick" farms.

RESOURCES

ces.ncsu.edu/depts/hort/hil/hil-8110.html: The North Carolina Extension Service has a great list of herbs, their space and light requirements, how to grow them, and uses.

GardenGuides.com: information on growing herbs

BARTENDER

14

Tending bar is a fun, creative, lucrative, and longstanding traditional business. You can become a bartender for events by working for a restaurant or catering business or offering your services to several catering businesses. Staff in the restaurant world turns over frequently, so you could also become a floating bartender who fills in for barkeeps on vacation or for establishments that are between bartenders.

If you can't tell chardonnay from cabernet and have never known what is in a Singapore Sling, don't despair. Bartending schools exist all over the country. In a few short weeks, you not only will know the ingredients of all the crazy-named drinks off the top of your head, but you will be able to pour an exact shot without using a measuring tool.

THINGS TO CONSIDER

Bartending often happens at night, so if you are not a night owl, this business may not be for you. There are ways, however, to do it without being out most of the night. You could focus on being a wedding bartender, as the majority of weddings happen during the day and early evening, so you would often be home by 9 p.m.

If you want to make considerable money as a bartender, you will also want to tend bar New Year's Eve and for holiday parties. Plan for the period between Thanksgiving and the new year to be very busy.

Also, depending on how you set up your business, you will want to be sure to check the liquor laws in the state in which you plan to operate.

Liquor sales are carefully controlled in all states and you need to take this aspect of this business seriously.

HOW DO YOU WANT TO SPEND YOUR DAY?

As a bartender, you can often spend your days lounging on the beach or sitting on the patio reading a book! There is not a lot of preparation involved. Unopened alcohol doesn't tend to spoil quickly so ordering supplies can be done at your convenience.

WHAT YOU WILL NEED

What you need for this business depends on the way in which you decide to operate. If you simply hire yourself out as a bartender to various restaurants, catering businesses, or even private parties, you will need little more than expertise. Bring along a good, up-to-date bartending recipe book or a smart phone that allows you internet access—people are always going to come up with that one drink you have never heard of. For private party work, you may need to provide not only the liquor but the wine, beer, and cocktail glasses. These can be rented or you can collect a supply of your own. And you will need a dishwasher to run them through after the event and before the next one.

MARKETING ANGLE

In this business, you will be marketing yourself. You need to be gregarious but not pushy. Part of marketing yourself will be to dress neatly and have excellent grooming. If you can concoct your own signature drink, so much the better. Anything that makes your potential client think "This person will make a great bartender and I no longer have to worry about this aspect of the party," is a great marketing tool.

NICE TOUCH

Some of the fun of being a bartender is experimenting with drinks. You may think that every drink under the sun has already been created, but you'd be surprised. New products—interesting beverages or juices and exotic ingredients—are brought to market all the time, making them a potential focus ingredient for stylish new cocktail.

EXPANSION POSSIBILITIES

If you become extremely proficient and desirable, you may want to expand and hire staff. You can send employees to do the more mundane bartending gigs, so you can keep the best ones for yourself.

You could also expand into offering tastings; wine, cocktail, or single-malt scotch, for example. You can either do this yourself and rent a venue—hold them regularly and create a kind of club—or you can team up with a restaurant to offer the tastings in conjunction with a dinner. Learn how to use alcohol in food recipes, and you will have yet another aspect added to your bartending career.

WORDS TO KNOW

Mixers: The sodas that are mixed with alcohol to make "mixed drinks."

Top shelf: A term that refers to name-brand alcohol, as apposed to lower-quality, less expensive "house" brands.

RESOURCES

bartending.com: an online community of bartenders
bartending.org: bartending schools, drink recipes, and online training.
webtender.com: drink recipes

15 COFFEE CART

Coffee is no longer relegated to breakfast. People are drinking coffee like never before. And everyone wants good coffee available everywhere at all times. As a result, having a coffee cart in a public place can be a very lucrative business. It won't take long to figure out the best times to be open for the location you have chosen. And the beauty of having a coffee cart is you can move it anywhere that seems like a better location, as long as you have the right permits.

THINGS TO CONSIDER

You could have a cart indoors in a big mall, but chances are you will be outdoors with your coffee cart, so you should like being outside. People have high expectations of coffee these days—gone are the days when customers accepted coffee that tasted like flavored hot water. We are even demanding that airlines provide a great cup of coffee! You need to plan to meet those expectations by using freshly ground, high-quality coffee, keeping it fresh, and having the right condiments to meet everyone's tastes.

HOW DO YOU WANT TO SPEND YOUR DAY?

As mentioned above, you will spend a lot of your day outdoors with a coffee cart. If you live in the northern part of the country, you probably won't be doing this in the winter months unless you find an indoor location for your cart. Look for malls that have a general entrance area that might have space for a cart.

WHAT YOU WILL NEED

A 6' x 3' cart starts around $4,000, which will quickly price you outside the $5,000 limit of this book. However, many companies lease carts; leasing would allow you to try different types of carts and establish your business before you actually purchase one.

The next important thing after a cart is to choose a source of coffee. Pick the highest-quality coffee roaster available. If there is a coffee business nearby, you can get freshly ground coffee daily, and you can support a local business at the same time. The roaster should be willing to include you as a source of their coffee on their marketing pieces.

MARKETING ANGLE

Choosing a local coffee supplier is a great marketing angle. If you can keep your prices a tad under the big-name chain coffee houses, that is another great angle. You will need to decide whether or not to sell more complicated coffee products such as latte and cappuccino; people have come to expect these types of coffees to be available everywhere coffee is sold, but another marketing tactic could be to not sell these and promote simplicity instead.

NICE TOUCH

Coffee, which is an enormous Latin/South American industry, is often identified with rainforests. Rainforests have long been decimated, mostly for wood products, but coffeemakers often align themselves with environmental efforts to save the rainforests and create sustainable practices for desirable rainforest products. You, too, can have your business support an environmental group—and let your customers know you do.

EXPANSION POSSIBILITIES

A basic expansion idea for a coffee cart is to add small food items to your menu. Typical would be pastries, bagels, toast, and the like. You could avoid the mainstream and perhaps offer European-style breakfast snacks such as cheese on great bread. You can also add chocolate bars for afternoon pick-me-ups.

WORDS TO KNOW

Caffeine: The chemical compound xanthine alkaloid, which acts as a mild stimulant.

Decaffeinated: Coffee with at least 97 percent of its original caffeine content removed.

Barista: Italian for bartender, a barista is someone who makes coffee drinks as a profession

Gourmet coffee: Sometimes called "specialty" or "premium" coffee, gourmet coffees are made from Arabica beans usually harvested by hand in mountainous areas. Gourmet coffees stand in stark contrast to the often bitter Robusta beans grown at low elevations and harvested by machine.

RESOURCES

breworganic.com
coffeecow.com
tea-and-coffee.com

LUNCH WAGON 16

A lunch wagon can be a fun and creative food-related business. And you will become popular wherever you set up shop. With a lunch wagon, you stock your wagon full of lunch foods and drinks and drive either to a central location where there are many offices within a short distance, or you drive around to several office buildings that are in relatively close proximity to each other over the course of a long lunch period. Depending on the kind of office buildings or manufacturing plants in your area, you might arrive at your first location at 11 a.m. and stay in one location for 45 minutes before you move on. You could get in three or even four locations each day.

Be sure to make your schedule very clear and stick to it, and workers will become accustomed to when you are in the area. Not everyone will buy their lunches from you every day, so those who are buying once a week won't mind that the time you stop at their workplace is 2 p.m. They may not want to eat lunch every day at that time, but once a week is fine.

This is where the lunch items you offer come into consideration. You can certainly have the typical hot dogs and other easy things to have on a lunch wagon, but you should also plan to have a few unique items—things that people can't resist having at least once or twice a week. After a stressful morning, they will be at your wagon to have that item they crave!

Another strategy is to find a business that will contract you to be in their parking lot. You drive there, set up shop, and stay for several hours. Shoppers can purchase lunch from you at their convenience.

Business people who get to know you are there will also remember you as a potential lunch spot—again, even more so if you carry unique and delicious lunch items. Big-box home-improvement centers and lumberyards are good places to try this idea, because contractors often use their lunch breaks to purchase materials.

Another approach to the lunch wagon is the breakfast wagon. You can use all the same approaches to find outlets for your wagon, just at a different time of day. In some instances, you can start as early as 5 a.m., depending on when shifts come and go or what kind of businesses an office building houses. Plan to run the breakfast route until around 11 a.m.

If you find a business that will let you set up shop in their parking lot, you can drive your rig there and leave it. Otherwise, you will need to have a place to park your lunch wagon at night. You will also need a vehicle that can haul it around.

As for your food choice, you can focus on the usual fare, like Italian sausage sandwiches, Greek gyros, or falafel sandwiches. Or you can offer a few new possibilities. These days, it is wise to offer a non-meat choice to attract vegetarian or minimal meat eating clientele. Be sure to have chips—even the most health-conscious eater can't avoid eating a few chips once in a while. Offer high-quality chips that are baked and therefore a little lower in calories. And, of course, you need at least a modest selection of drinks including regular and diet soda, bottled water, and iced tea or juice.

You need to be sure to clean your lunch wagon immaculately at the end of each day. Besides being subject to health considerations and regulations, no one will regularly visit an unclean food establishment. Being mobile presents unique challenges in the cleanliness department, but it is important to keep on top of it.

THINGS TO CONSIDER

Depending on the size and kind of lunch wagon you have, you may be outside a good portion of the day. Canopies can help keep you out of the elements. There may be some inclement days when you simply can't operate: not only would it be unpleasant for you, but chances are you wouldn't have enough customers to make it worthwhile anyway. Let your customers know your weather limitations: Post signs that say "Open every day except when raining hard or below 30 degrees" or something that gives them a pretty clear idea when you will be closed. Nothing frustrates customers more than to come to your establishment and find you closed.

HOW DO YOU WANT TO SPEND YOUR DAY?

This is not one of those behind-the-scenes food businesses. Lunch wagon clientele expect friendly service. If you are known to be "quite a character," this business will be perfect for you.

WHAT YOU WILL NEED

You will need a wagon. If you want to start right off big, you can lease or buy a used wagon that has cooking equipment and is designed so you are inside the wagon. This can make your business more full service, but it is a substantial financial commitment.

Starting off small is almost never a bad idea. You can always move up. Once you decide on which type of food you are going to focus, put together a basic inventory list and order your inventory.

MARKETING ANGLE

One marketing approach you can take with your lunch wagon is to offer healthy selections. You don't have to be extreme; just having lunch options that are not greasy, fried, and fattening will appeal to a lot of people. Make it all healthy and market it that way.

Before you make any marketing decision, however, be sure to test the waters of the workers you serve. If the office buildings on your route are filled with baby boomers, you could try adding a retro lunch to your menu, such as peanut butter and marshmallow Fluff sandwiches with a Ring Ding for dessert. But that isn't going to cut it with the boomers' kids, who are out there in the work force in as great a number as the boomers themselves. Get to know your clientele and choose your menu accordingly.

NICE TOUCH

Vary your menu every week, but don't change everything; if a day's new item doesn't appeal to someone, there should always be an old standby available that they know they like.

If you do choose the "healthy lunch" angle, be sure to have a couple of somewhat decadent dessert choices, such as oatmeal chocolate chip cookies or fruit and nut bars, to provide a satisfying but not over-the-top addition to a customer's healthy meal.

EXPANSION POSSIBILITIES

If you start small with a cart, you can always expand by continuing to upgrade your lunch vehicle. Keep in mind, however, whether there is enough business in your area to support a larger lunch service. Lunch wagons are always expandable by adding more wagons and more territories and routes, but since you can't be everywhere at once, this also means adding employees.

The ultimate expansion is to settle down and set up shop in a storefront space and create a real lunch restaurant. If you do this—a drastic move but certainly possible—you could also keep your lunch wagon route and have someone do it for you. If your restaurant is in the same territory, you could direct your current wagon customers to your restaurant and create a new territory for the wagon.

WORDS TO KNOW

Generator: a gasoline or propane engine that provides electrical power to run appliances remotely.

Diner: What we today commonly think of as a classic shiny silver eat-in restaurant was originally designed to be a mobile lunch wagon.

RESOURCES

carriageworks.com

supremeproducts.com: suppliers of vending carts

vendingtrucks.com

$$

17 COOKWARE SALES

Cooking is more fun and more successful with the right equipment. Even people who cook only casually realize the advantages of having good cookware. Kitchen shops are popular, but sometimes the cookware gets lost in the crowd of linens, candles, and small appliances. A small business focused solely on cookware can be a standout in the crowd.

Search for the best quality cookware on the market that is suitable for the average to above-average chef. You can certainly look online but the best way to find what you want to sell is to be able to pick pieces up and even use them in hands-on demonstrations and classes.

One way to condense your search is to attend a cooking trade show. Many cookware manufacturers will be there with booths that showcase their cookware. Great discounts are often offered at trade shows if you order at the show. Often these deals include free shipping, which can be a cost-effective way to help set up shop.

In retail, suppliers often require new customers to pay cash for their first purchase before setting up an account. But at a trade show, the rules often can be bent. Manufacturers spend a lot of money to exhibit at trade shows, not only for the booth space, but for all the booth accoutrements, ads in the program, and especially for travel and housing expense to send people to staff the booth. The salespeople are often handed sales quotas to meet, which often includes not just dollar amounts but also new accounts. They are hungry to meet those quotas, so use that to your advantage.

This doesn't mean you should purchase willy nilly. Set aside a certain amount of your startup budget to pay up front for inventory, particularly if the manufacturer offers a better discount at trade shows and especially with those items that you know will be sure sellers. Take on some "flyers" or products on a returnable basis—things that you aren't sure will sell, or items that are new for the manufacturer and for which they do not have a track record. You won't get as good of a discount on returnable merchandise, but you also won't be stuck with it if it doesn't sell. If the item does prove to sell well in your store, reorder on a nonreturnable basis with a better discount.

Trade shows can be spellbinding, so be sure to go in with a plan. What do you need to set up shop? Literally, map out your retail space (which should be relatively small to start with) and keep the map with you at all times. What kind of display is on each wall? What kind of floor display do you have or need? Tabletops? Find a couple of manufacturers that lend display units with their merchandise. Usually, the first time out, that requires that you purchase enough merchandise to fill the display, but don't forget that you will have saved the cost of a display unit for your new shop.

Setting up a retail space can quickly get way beyond the $5,000 startup limits of this book. But if you start small and look for creative ways to fill your space, you can do it. Perhaps half the space is taken up initially with a demonstration/class area—basically a tabletop with perhaps a built-in stovetop. Don't be afraid to start small and build your business as you go.

THINGS TO CONSIDER

Be creative in how you get your retail space set up. Negotiate with your landlord to do things such as the renovation and electrical work needed for your cooking class area as "leasehold improvements." It is to your landlord's benefit that your business succeeds; retail has a high failure rate, and landlords hate having empty space, so develop a great relationship and get your landlord to work with you.

HOW DO YOU WANT TO SPEND YOUR DAY?

The thing about retail is that you are committed to your shop for long hours almost every day. There are two ways to combat that.

1. Make sure to give yourself a couple of days off. Working seven days a week, 12 hours a day is a surefire recipe for quick burnout. Find ways to keep it fresh—and one way is to recharge yourself regularly by making the time to do the other things you love to do.

2. As soon as you can, hire someone to relieve you in the store. Teach this person how to run the store, deal with customers, etc., but in the beginning, think of this person as a warm body who can keep the store open and the cash register jingling when you are not there. Then you can concentrate on setting up the cooking classes, figuring out how to market your business, and doing research on your competition.

Also, plan to overlap with your employee at least a couple times each week. This allows you to get to know him or her a little, it gives you a feeling of collegiality, and it allows you to teach this employee about the store and get him or her excited about being part of your venture.

WHAT YOU WILL NEED

You will need a retail space. It is possible to do cookware sales as "home parties;" this may be a way to start your business and collect some funds, but you will need to focus on just one type of cookware.

You will need some display equipment. This can be racks or simply tables. Be creative with display; avoid items that require very specific display space unless the manufacturer provides the display unit or materials at no cost to you. Simple hooks screwed into the wall and tables covered with nice tablecloths or edged fabric pieces are just fine. Allow the cookware itself to decorate your store, not fancy display ware.

You will need a cash register and the ability to accept all types of credit cards.

MARKETING ANGLE

Get people in your store with cooking classes. If you can offer them at no charge, great. If you need to pay someone to conduct the classes, charge just enough to cover the cost of the instructor's fee plus the food items needed for the demonstration. Focus the classes around one cooking tool, perhaps a particular pan, and give everyone in the class a 10 percent discount coupon to purchase that pan within a month's time. Offer an even better discount if they purchase the item before they leave the class. If they do and they love it, they can use their 10 percent coupon to come back and buy one as a gift or, even better, give the coupon to a friend to come to your store to purchase their own. That way, you get two sales and a new customer!

NICE TOUCH

Become known as the go-to person for special cookware items. Professional cooks and school programs can come to you for ordering. You can even let individual customers look at catalogs (without the pricing, since catalogs will typically include what your cost would be, not theirs), which can inspire them to order things that they might not even know exist.

EXPANSION POSSIBILITIES

Once you are established, expansion with a retail store is easy. Start to add accessory items to complement your cookware. These can be important items since customers who may not be ready to drop a few hundred dollars on a complete cookware set may walk out with $50 worth of utensils or cookbooks.

Talk with book publishers about having cookbook authors come to a book signing and give a free demonstration or class as part of the signing event.

WORDS TO KNOW

Phenolic: A heat-resistant plastic.

Satin and sunray finishes: Satin finishes are applied to the bottoms of pans by brushing to provide better heat absorption. Sunray is an abrasive finish done with sandpaper while the pan is rotating.

RESOURCES

cookware.org: The Cookware Manufacturers Association is a nonprofit trade organization for cookware manufacturers

mitechtrading.com: cookware wholesaler

WINEMAKING

18

Winemaking is a romantic and slow process. Although owning your own vineyards and cultivating your own grapes is a lovely idea, it is beyond the scope of this book. However, you can purchase grapes to make your wines. And there are many wines that can be made with things other than grapes. Winemakers have experimented with dandelion greens, elderberries, apples, and many other fruits and berries. These often result in tasty but heavy and sweet wines that are best suited as "dessert wines." If you want to make sip-with-cheese wine or wine to be partaken of over dinner, you need to make wine from grapes.

Your first task will be to locate a grape distributor and determine how to place an order. When the grapes are ready—an unpredictable moment, at best—they will be picked and they will be delivered to you. Approximately 70 pounds of grapes makes approximately five gallons of wine.

When the approximate picking time approaches, you need to be ready to receive your grapes and start the winemaking process! First you must prepare yeast (a type specific to winemaking, not brewer's or baker's yeast), which converts the natural sugars in the crushed grapes to alcohol.

When the grapes arrive, be prepared to sort and wash them. To make wine, grapes are crushed, and to do this, you will need a crushing machine. Plan to rent one rather than buy it up front.

Next there are several stages of filtering and siphoning and fermenting and bottling. Winemaking is a complex process and not a business for the weak of heart!

THINGS TO CONSIDER

Being involved in the alcohol business is a major undertaking. You need to be up to date on every possible law and rule there is regarding alcohol in your state, and the federal laws as well. These laws can be very peculiar; you may need some experienced help to interpret them. The liquor commissioner for your state can probably walk you through the legal requirements for whatever you have planned.

Also, you need to enjoy being a bit of a chemist to make wine. Important things such as specific gravity, acidity, and fermentation will become second nature to you.

There is a bit of equipment involved; none is outrageously expensive, and much of it can be rented until you decide whether this is a business for you or not.

HOW DO YOU WANT TO SPEND YOUR DAY?

Comparatively speaking, very little of your time will be spent actually making wine. While grapes are fermenting and wine is aging, you should spend a lot of your time marketing your product.

If you like to work by yourself or (depending how big your business gets) with just a small number of people, this may be a great business for you.

WHAT YOU WILL NEED

For the business as a whole, you will need a grape press, a fermentor, hydrometer, and bottling equipment, including a corker. For each batch, you will need bottles and corks, as well as other items such as yeast, bentonite (brown powder added to the wine to clarify it), sulphite (for sterilizing equipment), and isinglass (a clearing agent).

You will also need some space to do all this. The good news is that if you need to rent space, it doesn't need to be in a high-rent neighborhood and it doesn't need much in the way of accoutrements. If you want to sell your wine in a storefront, you can carve out a small portion of the space and have a little retail area. You could also have some fun with wine tastings and perhaps some classes on how to cook with wine.

MARKETING ANGLE

One of the most important marketing aspects of your wine will be your name and the resulting label for your wine bottles. Lots of effort and creative thought go into wine labeling. The name you choose should sound appealing. Wine tends to be a distinguished business and choosing a name that has a distinguished sound is important. You may want to choose the name of a local geographical feature or some concept that is associated with your region—e.g., "Liberty Wine" for the Philadelphia area or "Gateway Wine" for the St. Louis area.

NICE TOUCH

Small wine businesses need to promote the mom-and-pop aspect of their winemaking. Vintners get downright sentimental about their personal process of winemaking and the care and attention that goes into each bottle of wine. Perhaps include a tag on the neck of the bottle that explains how you started the business, what you love about it, what you love about this particular wine, and so on.

EXPANSION POSSIBILITIES

If you start small—and you should—you can always make more wine, offer winemaking classes, do seasonal wine tastings, and expand in simple ways on the small business you have started.

WORDS TO KNOW

Tannins: A chemical produced from the fermentation of stems left on the grapes. The stems can add flavor; it's for the vintner to decide.

Vinification: The process of making wine.

RESOURCES

northeastwinemaking.com: Northeast Produce Inc. is a distributor of winemaking equipment and grapes.

winemakinginfo-online.com

FOOD GIFT BASKETS   19

Gift baskets are a perennial good business; there's always a demand. The most common gift baskets are assembled using food items. You can sell your gift baskets via a retail store or a website, or preferably both. A retail store will restrict you to local business; a website will give you the whole country, if not the world, as a potential customer base.

If you lease a retail storefront, you can make it multi-use by using it to put together your baskets. But you have to be attentive to walk-in customers too, so only you can decide whether this is a good idea or not. A lot will depend on where you set up your shop. If it is in a major retail location, be prepared for considerable walk-in traffic, mostly in the form of window shoppers.

THINGS TO CONSIDER

This can be big business, but it needs a lot of marketing; there is a lot of competition out there!

The best way to get the best prices on your supplies is to buy in bulk. One way to do that is to have a specialty, so you will buy a lot of a certain product, such as chocolate or coffee or a specific candy. Don't try to spread yourself too thin and make dozens of different kinds of baskets. You can always customize with one or two items, but it's best to standardize most of the basket's contents.

Another thing to consider when creating food-related gift baskets is whether you are going to use perishable foods or not. The main repercussion of this is you will pass higher delivery costs along to your customers, because the baskets will need to be delivered via overnight courier. You also need to be sure the recipient will be available to accept the delivery if it includes items that need to be refrigerated.

HOW DO YOU WANT TO SPEND YOUR DAY?

You will spend a lot of your day producing gift baskets and packing them for shipping. This is a demanding kind of work, and while some of it can be done at a high table while you sit on a bar stool, you will find you are constantly getting up for this or that since probably everything won't be within reach.

WHAT YOU WILL NEED

You will need an excellent workspace with plenty of room, a large worktable, shelving for organized storage, and easy access to supplies such as scissors, tape, cellophane rolls, ribbon, and your ingredients for your baskets.

You may need a few pieces of equipment such as a heat sealer. And you will need to have the ability to accept credit cards.

If you decide to have a storefront, you will need display furniture and a checkout counter, as well as an inventory of pre-made baskets for purchase and for samples.

MARKETING ANGLE

Your best marketing angle will be to specialize in a certain style of gift basket. You can always branch out from there, but to be able to start your business, especially for less than $5,000, you will need to keep your startup expenses to a minimum.

NICE TOUCH

A nice touch in any delivery business is to include an e-mail to the person who ordered the gift basket to tell them their order has been sent.

EXPANSION POSSIBILITIES

The expansion possibilities with the gift basket business are endless. If you start small with just a couple of gift basket selections, you can always start to mix and match the contents, and offer different-size baskets that expand the selection with each increase in size.

WORDS TO KNOW

Anchoring: Securing items in a basket so they don't tumble around during delivery.

Shred: The filler used to line the bottom of the basket.

RESOURCES

festivities-pub.com: website for *Gift Basket Review* magazine
giftwarenews.com

20 PERSONAL CHEF

There are a number of reasons why someone would want a personal chef. According to the Private & Personal Chef Association, the most common group of people to hire a personal chef (who works with a number of clients, as opposed to a private chef who works for just one client) are "two-income couples with or without children, career-focused individuals, those with special dietary or health needs, seniors, and those who enjoy fine dining." Whatever the reason, if you have the credentials, this can be a rewarding food-related business venture. The industry has been growing and, according to the AAPCA, the number of personal chefs is supposed to double over the next five years.

THINGS TO CONSIDER

Clients who hire personal chefs are picky by design. Personal chefs are hired to solve a problem, such as creating quality meals for people too busy to cook for themselves or for people who have special dietary needs. Solving problems for people with something as personal as food can be fraught with potential issues.

The biggest way to avoid issues of any kind is communication. Create very open communication with your clients to completely understand their needs, desires, and tastes. And keep those lines of communication open at all times—don't assume anything.

HOW DO YOU WANT TO SPEND YOUR DAY?

Being a personal chef can be a very demanding way to make a living.

However, it is also very diverse. You will create menus, research recipes, shop for the very best ingredients, and learn about your clients' needs, expectations, and preferences. The variety of clients will also add to this interesting work life. Unless you decide to specialize in one aspect of personal chef service, you will be able to have clients with varying needs.

WHAT YOU WILL NEED

This is not a high-cost startup business. You may use your clients' kitchen or, depending on what kind of service you provide, you may use your own kitchen and package meals for your clients.

MARKETING ANGLE

One way to market yourself as a personal chef is to focus on one aspect of the service, such as providing meals for those with special dietary needs or families with little time for meal-making but with a desire to have great meals, or for those who can simply afford to pay to have someone take care of meal preparation. If you target a specific market, you can focus your efforts on how to service that kind of client.

NICE TOUCH

You will get to know your clients and figure out interesting ways to stretch your service to them beyond just the expected. Look for details about their personal interests and things they care about. For example, if you make meals for a diabetic grandmother and you know on her eight-year-old grandson comes to stay with her a couple afternoons a week after school, include a couple homemade cookies wrapped and marked with his name. Or if someone is under some unusual stress, include a relaxing tea with their meal. Little touches go a long way.

EXPANSION POSSIBILITIES

The expansion possibilities are a little difficult with this type of personal service. You can work toward developing menus that can be replicated and have people work for you. But there are only so many clients you can take on and still give the personal service that your clients will expect. As you become better known and clients come and go, you can add new clients at higher costs.

Another possibility is to keep a few prime clients while you also create a general business that provides personal meals to a broad clientele—sort of a high-level "meals to go" business.

WORDS TO KNOW

Concierge: A staff member at a hotel or resort who helps guests make tour reservations, obtain reservations, and attends to miscellaneous guest needs.

Diet: The usual food and drink that a person consumes; daily sustenance. A healthy diet consists of appropriate portions of the five food groups, avoiding deep-fried items, and eating fresh foods whenever possible.

Menu: An entire meal, as opposed to the individual items.

RESOURCES

culinarybusiness.com: Culinary Business Academy

hireachef.com: a website that allows potential clients to search for a personal chef in their area.

personalchef.com: American Personal & Private Chef Association

CHOCOLATE MAKING **21**

Chocolate is a perennial food favorite. Chocolate lovers are always willing to try a new version of their preferred food group.

Chocolate is a pretty crowded food business—perhaps you've heard of Hershey, Mars, Lindt, or Ghirardelli—to break into so you will want to be sure to create some way to stand out right from the beginning. First, you will need to make superb chocolate. Second, something about your chocolate needs to be unique. That uniqueness can be the confection itself. Or it can be unique packaging. It can even be a unique name that relates to a charitable cause to which a portion of the proceeds goes.

Making candy to sell from chocolate is the endpoint in a somewhat arduous process. According to the "chocolate" entry in Wikipedia, the cacao beans are harvested, removed from their pods, and fermented for as much as a week before they are spread out to dry. The beans are then shelled and the nibs removed. The nibs are ground to produce chocolate liquor, which is the starting point for what the chocolate will become.

This is where you come in. Once you decide what kind of chocolate you want to make—dark, milk, and white all require different additional ingredients—you will need to decide what else you will put in your chocolates before it is poured into a mold. Nuts, fruit, jellies, liquors, and other flavorings are all possibilities.

You will want to have a website, of course, but be aware that shipping chocolate needs some special handling, particularly during the summer months. You don't want your confections to melt before they get to their destination. Many chocolate suppliers insist on shipping express methods and/or with cold packs to help keep them from melting.

THINGS TO CONSIDER

Making artisan-style chocolate is a time consuming business. However, the creative aspect of it can make up for the attention you need to pay to detail. But if you aren't the super-focused type, this may not be the business for you.

HOW DO YOU WANT TO SPEND YOUR DAY?

Making chocolate is an indoor business. But it can also be done any time of the day or night, so you can set your own hours. How many hours you want to put into it depends on how big you want your business to be.

WHAT YOU WILL NEED

The foundation of chocolate is the cacao bean. Chocolate typically comes in dark, milk, and white versions (although white is not considered true chocolate). You will need milk, sugar, flavorings, and fillings. And you will need candy molds to create your chocolate candies.

If you want to use real chocolate for your candies, you will need to temper it before you pour it into molds in order to prevent the butter crystals from losing their suspension and creating white streaks on the surface of your candies. The process for tempering is time consuming but not difficult.

MARKETING ANGLE

This is the kind of food business where marketing the local angle can be crucial; you can have a great business just selling chocolate locally.

Packaging is also important. Chocolate and other candy makers are constantly trying to create the next new thing. You can't miss a York Peppermint Patty. SkyBars have their funky (and delicious!) separate pouches with different fillings in each. Hershey's, of course, has the Kiss. Chocolate seems to crave creative presentation.

Taking a page from the big guys' playbook is not a bad idea. You don't have to spend all your startup funds on some impossibly difficult way to create your chocolate. But you can stand out with a striking package or other unique touch.

NICE TOUCH

You might be able to get more shops to carry your artisan chocolates if you provide a simple display unit for them. This is also a great way to get retail outlets to order a set amount—and when the display unit starts to look a little empty, they are more inclined to reorder to replenish the display unit.

EXPANSION POSSIBILITIES

Once you have perfected your creation, you can hire someone to make the candies for you while you start to experiment with new recipes and new ideas for your next line of chocolates.

You can also start to expand your market area as soon as you are able to create the volume of chocolate needed to supply it.

WORDS TO KNOW

Conching: A grinding-like process that makes chocolate the smooth texture most of us are familiar with.

Tempering: Technique used to stabilize chocolate through a melting and cooling process so it will set firm and be shiny at room temperature.

Theobromine: An alkaloid present in chocolate that is considered to have health benefits for humans but is toxic to cats and dogs.

RESOURCES

anoccasionalchocolate.com: a candy-making supply company

onestopcandle.com: a chocolate and candy-making supply company

VEGETABLE STAND

22

L ike many food-related businesses, today's food consumer wants to purchase as many locally grown and produced foods as possible. Many vegetables are easy to grow and can easily be sold from an old-fashioned farm or vegetable stand.

THINGS TO CONSIDER

Marketing your vegetables as organic is a popular thing to do these days, but to be "certified organic" is a long, complex, and sometimes expensive process. Don't promote yourself as organic unless your farm has been certified as such. However, that doesn't mean you can't promote the fact that you don't use pesticides and do things such as rotate crops, use nontoxic pest control, and other organic-type procedures.

HOW DO YOU WANT TO SPEND YOUR DAY?

Farming of any kind, including growing vegetables in enough quantity to make a business out of it, involves physical labor. You need to be in excellent physical shape to prepare your vegetable beds as well as plant and weed. Not only is this work physical, but it is outdoor work as well. Bugs and rain can't slow you down. But if all that doesn't scare you, then it might just be the right business for you.

WHAT YOU WILL NEED

You will need a plot of land to grow some vegetables; if you don't have your own property to do this, you may be able to lease some space from someone who does. To grow those vegetables, you will need seeds and plants. If you have some indoor space to start seeds, you can start even slow-growing vegetables from seed early in the season.

Use only the best quality seed from top-notch seed companies—there's no point in wasting your time and labor on low-quality crops. Depending on the soil, you may need some type of fertilizer. But be sure to start with good soil and work in good composted material before planting. Some plants, such as tomatoes, beans, peas, and cucumbers, need some structural support, which not only helps the vine-like plants climb, but it also keeps the fruit off the ground and saves space.

You'll need to get water to your garden in the event of a dry spell. This is particularly important shortly after planting.

Before even planting the first seed, have a plan for how you will deal with pests. Bugs have a way of finding a direct path to the garden. Pests can get out of hand quickly, so you want to be proactive. Every vegetable has a particular insect or two that especially likes them, so you must be prepared.

When you sell any foodstuff to the public, it needs to look almost perfect. The same goes for fresh vegetables. No—or few—digs, nicks, or dark spots. The shapes should be even and uniform.

Have some baskets ready to harvest your crops and get them to your vegetable stand. You can sell them at a roadside stand at your home or you can look for a farmer's market close by where you can sell your vegetables. If neither of those is a possibility, ask a local business if you can use their parking lot and sell from the back of a truck or under a canopy with a couple of tables set up.

MARKETING ANGLE

Definitely use the "locally grown" marketing angle wherever possible. People are beginning to care a great deal about knowing where their food comes from and how it was grown and handled.

NICE TOUCH

Sell well-made baskets that customers can bring back to fill with vegetables. Make up a set "menu" that the basket can hold and give it a set price—something like four tomatoes, two cukes, a couple onions, a summer squash, a clump of radishes, some peas or green beans, and a baggie of an herb of their choice for $10. And change it slightly each week as things come in and out of season.

EXPANSION POSSIBILITIES

Selling fresh vegetables from your garden, although rewarding, is not a huge moneymaking venture. There are ways to expand, however, that can bring in higher profits. Think about what small steps you can take to broaden your scope. You could can some vegetables and sell them for a higher price—the higher price, however, also includes your time because canning is a time-consuming process. Consider selling things such as pickles, relishes, and jams since they don't entail the same food safety issues as other canned products. Also, you can create products from your vegetables and sell them.

Consider focusing on a type of produce that a local restaurant might use. Spend the winter season interviewing restaurant owners to find out if there is an herb or particular vegetable you might grow for them.

You can also look into opening a year-round, indoor farm stand. Start making connections with other gardeners and expand your offering to include flowers and carving pumpkins, gourds, and Christmas wreaths and trees.

WORDS TO KNOW

Organic: "Certified organic" produce meets rigorous federal criteria that include a several-year process of using only natural fertilizers and pest-control methods.

CSA: Community-supported Agriculture, referring to "subscription" gardens where people pay up front to be provided with a weekly allotment of produce throughout the growing season.

Hybrid: A cross between two varieties, often done to utilize the best qualities of each variety, such as large plant and resistance to disease.

RESOURCES

ccof.org: California Certified Organic Farmers
farmersmarket.com: national directory of farmer's markets
midwestorganic.com
organicconsumers.org: Organic Farmers and Gardeners Union

PIZZA STAND

Pizza is a perennial favorite and will always find a market, if made well. While pizza ovens can be expensive, you can't go wrong selling this delicious meal to the public.

It will be difficult to have a full pizza oven out on the sidewalk. So a pizza stand can take a few possible approaches. The easiest way would be to purchase pizzas from a local pizza house and use a warmer at your pizza stand to reheat them and keep them warm. Then you can sell pizza by the slice. You will need to have at least three different kinds: a meat pizza, an all-vegetable pizza, and a plain cheese pizza. This way you deal with none of the fuss of actually making pizza.

Another thing you might do is sell personal-size pizzas. Again, these should be in at least three different varieties to accommodate all tastes. You won't be able to make these pizzas from scratch at your stand, unless you decide to have an indoor takeout pizza stand instead of a sidewalk stand—but you could make them ahead of time and either cook or reheat them at the stand.

Pizza is a self-contained meal, so you won't need to sell much else besides a selection of drinks. Like the pizza, you don't have to get fancy; most people can be satisfied with three or four different types of drinks: soda, diet soda, bottled water, and a non-soda drink such as juice or iced tea.

THINGS TO CONSIDER

This is an on-your-feet kind of job. And it can be in the heat, out on the sidewalk with a heating source right beside you. If the heat gets to you, this is not a business for you. On the other hand, during the cooler seasons, it can be quite pleasant.

HOW DO YOU WANT TO SPEND YOUR DAY?

This food-related business puts you right out there with the public, unless you want to be the behind-the-scenes person making the pizzas and not selling them, which is possible if you hire someone to run the stand for you. But in the beginning, as with almost all businesses, you will want to do it all. Not only does this avoid your having to pay your revenue out to employees, but it also gives you a complete sense of every aspect of your business so you always know how to do everything, what needs to be done, what the complexities are, and what are realistic expectations.

WHAT YOU WILL NEED

You will need to either locate in a place where you have access to a significant power source, or you need a gas-powered heating oven. You will need covered cases for your pizzas to be displayed, even if it's just a piece of each kind. You'll need a cash box or a small register. Behind the scenes, you will need the basic pizza ingredients—flour for dough and various ingredients depending on the types of pizzas you choose to offer—and the ability to make the pizzas. Or you need a relationship with a pizza maker to supply you with the pizza that you need.

MARKETING ANGLE

Pizza has a way of selling itself. The street vendor/food-stand type business is one that attracts attention with aromas and by providing quick, convenient, appetizing fast food. But you should pay attention to details such as your business name, which can be a great marketing tool, especially for word-of-mouth marketing; and to the quality of your product, which is always the most important food-related business marketing tool. Keep your signage neat and don't make your business too complex. People eat at a street stand to keep things simple.

NICE TOUCH

Offer a package meal—two slices of pizza and a drink for a set price. Don't make it too confusing; your customers just want a simple lunch. And you don't want to spend much time cashing people out, you want to be selling to the next customer.

EXPANSION POSSIBILITIES

One way you could expand this business is to have a few vendors around a metro area. If your business name becomes familiar enough to people, they will patronize your pizza stand anywhere, the same way they do brick-and-mortar chain restaurants around the country.

WORDS TO KNOW

Reconditioned: used equipment (in this case, pizza ovens) that have been remanufactured or reconditioned so they are almost like new.

Epicurean: relating to the pursuit of pleasure, often used as an adjective for artisan foods

Fermentation: dough contains yeast that has gone through a chemical process known as fermentation, which caused air bubbles and made the dough "rise."

RESOURCES

leaseithere.com: restaurant equipment leasing
northernpizzaequipment.com

24 JUICE DRINKS

Yum. Juice drinks can be nutritious and delicious. With the continuing trend toward health-conscious eating, juice bars can be lucrative and fairly uncomplicated businesses.

Although uncomplicated, there are three important aspects to this business that need to be learned.

1. **The recipes.** You can experiment and create some completely unique drinks; you can use existing recipes for drinks that are known to be good sellers; or you can take existing recipes and find ways to alter them to make them unique to you, but you need juice drink recipes. Some combination of all three is a great place to start.

2. **Preparing the drinks.** No matter in what form you decide to sell your products—either already made and bottled or made on demand—you will need to make the drinks. You can do both the recipe selection and creation, as well as the actual drink making, at least at first. But once you develop a following, you will become too busy to do both.

3. **Selling your drinks.** This can be done in a multitude of ways—from a vending stand, as part of someone else's business, like a local convenience store, or by selling bottled products to retailers.

Of course, you will also need to do the things that every business must do—marketing, advertising, bookkeeping, and keeping your food preparation and sales areas immaculately clean. Once again, it pays to start small and expand when you're ready rather than getting in overwhelmed from the start.

THINGS TO CONSIDER

Fruits are highly perishable. Being in a food business can be stressful enough, but when you are working with products that will go bad this quickly, you need to learn to order just the right quantities. And you need to learn how to handle fruit so it stays fresh and edible as long as possible.

Although you want to use only the highest-quality fruit, it is not critical that it be completely free of dings and nicks because you won't be selling the fruit in its original state. And being just slightly overripe can be a good thing, because most very ripe fruits will be juicier and give a stronger flavor to the drink.

HOW DO YOU WANT TO SPEND YOUR DAY?

Juice drinks can be messy! You will spend your day creating sticky wet products. If you like things perfectly neat, this may not be the business for you. However, being neat with any food business is critical, so maybe you would enjoy keeping this business under control.

WHAT YOU WILL NEED

You will need to decide what kinds of juice drinks you will serve and create a menu for your customers to choose from. You will need the specific ingredients that make these drinks the speciality that they are. Also, you will need the basis for all of your drinks, which could be anything from water to ice to yogurt, cow's milk, soy milk, concentrated juices, apple juice, cranberry juice, or your own secret combination.

MARKETING ANGLE

Juice drinks are viewed as healthy. While you can't make specific health claims, you can use marketing tactics that imply healthful living with your juices. Use wholesome, healthy-looking colors and images, such as healthy-looking people jogging, walking in the woods, bicycling, and, of course, drinking what appears to be your juice drinks!

Promote your drinks as a great start to the morning: If you have a kiosk, you want people to start their day with your drinks. They should also consider your juice for a midmorning energy boost, a refreshing drink to have with a healthy lunch, and as a pick-me-up in the afternoon. You want them to think of your juice drinks any time of the day.

NICE TOUCH

Have some drinks on your menu that have specific targeted purposes, such as an energy drink or have specific vitamins that are known to have certain properties (for example, Vitamin D has been in the news lately as an important vitamin for women fighting breast cancer). Soy products are recommended for menopausal women, although you will need to market that carefully.

EXPANSION POSSIBILITIES

If you have come up with a unique juice drink, one huge way to expand is to bottle it and sell it to retail outlets. The beverage industry is enormous and controlled by just a few big players, but it has happened many times before that a drink company—often started in someone's kitchen—that becomes locally popular is sold to one of the big beverage companies for a tidy sum. Certainly don't count on this happening, but being creative and devising a unique drink can have a decent payoff.

WORDS TO KNOW

Smoothie: A blended, chilled, and usually sweet drink made from fresh fruit and pureed to be smooth and typically thick.

Lo-fat: Low fat cooking refers to finding ways to make foods that reduces the amount of fat in the final product.

Nutritional supplements: Smoothies often contain supplements such as wheat germ or brewer's yeast that can make them more nutritional and are easily blended in.

RESOURCES

healthysmoothierecipe.net

thefruitpages.com

25 FRESH PASTA

Lots of foods come and go, but pasta is a dish that never seems to go out of style. Fresh pasta is far better than the pasta you buy in boxes at the grocery store. If you can make pasta and get it in the hands of busy people on their way home from work, you can have a solid business.

Like with any business, you should research your area to be sure there isn't another fresh pasta maker already selling in the territory you would target. Not that similar companies don't compete with each other all the time, but you don't need to walk into established competition with your startup business.

Pasta itself is comprised of just three ingredients: flour, egg, and salt. To make commercial quantities, you will need to find a large-size recipe or experiment making large portions of a smaller recipe. Simply doubling or tripling a recipe doesn't always work, so you will need to experiment to find the right recipes for the amounts you want to make. Other ingredients depend on your creativity—spinach, pesto, and tomato-basil pasta are all popular flavors.

As with most homemade foods, you will want to use only the very best ingredients. Consumers expect homemade foods to surpass store-bought, prepackaged foods in almost every way including freshness, taste, quality of ingredients, and even packaging. You will not stand out in the crowd or be able to command the prices you need to charge for your boutique products if you do not live up to this quality. And you don't want to make pasta for your business using the little home dinner-quantity-size machine sold at kitchen stores. Pricing for commercial pasta makers at the time of this writing included a manual pasta maker with an output of 30 pounds per hour for less than $1,000. Electric models were closer to $2,000. Most pasta makers come with the basic machine for rolling the dough and an attachment for cutting. Attachments for different sizes allow you to make the different kinds of pasta such as linguine, fettuccini, and angel hair.

If you make your pasta in your home kitchen, it is best to be able to dedicate an area exclusively to pasta making. Given that pasta making doesn't require much in the way of complicated equipment, you could even easily turn a separate room into the pasta business. A small refrigerator can store a week's supply of eggs. Flour needs just a sealed container. Having a water supply and sink in the room is helpful for keeping things clean but this renovation can be done as your business grows. If you choose to use an electric pasta maker, you will need a power supply, but this does not have to be anything out of the ordinary. Finally, be sure to have excellent task lighting focused on your work areas.

You can extend your pasta's shelf life if you invest in a vacuum sealer. Refrigerated vacuum-sealed pasta can last as long as six weeks.

THINGS TO CONSIDER

Selling fresh pasta is a business fraught with the dangers of perishables. Fresh pasta lasts only so long on the refrigerator shelf. You need to account for inevitable spoilage in your business plan and revenue forecasting. Although you will learn how to make and order your fresh foods to minimize spoilage, it is simply a fact of life in the food business. When calculating how much to make, remember that it is better to run out and be in demand than to throw away your hard-made product at the end of the day.

HOW DO YOU WANT TO SPEND YOUR DAY?

Making pasta can be a peaceful business. Kneading dough is relaxing and, if you use a manual dough roller and cutter, the only noise you need to hear is the chirping of birds outside the window or your favorite music playing in the background.

WHAT YOU WILL NEED

You will need your pasta recipes in place before you start your first batch of pasta. From there, you will need appropriate supplies of unbleached flour, eggs, and salt, depending on how much pasta per day you plan to make to start or need to make.

Although you can make pasta without a pasta maker instead using just a rolling pin and a knife (and this "free form pasta" might be a great marketing angle!), you should plan to acquire a pasta maker that has a roller and cutting attachments. Look on any of the online auction or sales sites and you can probably pick up a used machine.

MARKETING ANGLE

Spend time coming up with a unique and creative name for your pasta business. Customers remember names, and they like telling their friends about the quaint-sounding brand of pasta they found. The name needs to be pronounceable and memorable all at the same time. While it is best if the name includes the fact that the business is all about pasta—Pasta-Rama, for instance—it isn't totally necessary, but your marketing job will be a tad more challenging if you have to make sure people relate the name "Redonzo" with homemade pasta.

NICE TOUCH

It is always a nice touch to provide recipe ideas with any food ingredient. Change your recipe ideas each week, rotate them every few months, and give customers fresh ideas for ways to serve your pasta. Of course, use the sauces that you will inevitably make to accompany your pastas in all of your recipes. And consider collecting the recipes all together to create a Pasta-Rama Cookbook!

EXPANSION POSSIBILITIES

One of the most logical expansion possibilities with a pasta business is to also sell the sauces that might accompany your pastas. Tomato-based sauces and cheese sauces are perhaps the most popular. If you can get a handle on your pasta-making and perhaps train someone to do it as well as you do, you can begin to explore the sauce angle and add that to your repertoire.

You will need to make sure that the retail outlets that sell your pastas have the space and interest to also sell your sauces. You could also sell mail order via your website, although you will want to charge for premium shipping so the fresh pasta doesn't linger in transit very long.

WORDS TO KNOW

Al dente: An Italian term that indicates pasta is cooked to the point of being "firm to the bite."

Durum: A type of wheat grown in the midwestern U.S. that has a golden color and a good firmness for good cooking quality.

Semolina: The middle portion of durum wheat which is purified to make pastas

RESOURCES

pastabiz.com: professional pasta machines

recipetips.com: recipes for homemade pasta

26 SEAFOOD SALES

$$

Seafood sales can be a tricky business, but it also can be lucrative if you pull all the right pieces together. First, you will need a top-quality, reliable supplier for each kind of seafood you plan to sell. Second, whether you sell on the side of the road or sell seafood to restaurants and grocery stores, you will need a refrigerated truck. Buying one will be too expensive for the startup phase, so plan to lease one for a while until you grow your business and save some funds to purchase one.

THINGS TO CONSIDER

This is a highly perishable food business, and you need the stamina to not be stressed out by this fact. You may find for the first few weeks you are tossing more product than you can bear, but you will better understand your customers' sales cycles and what quantities to order.

Seafood sales can also be a stinky business—some people love the smell, some don't. You—and your family—should be the former.

HOW DO YOU WANT TO SPEND YOUR DAY?

The biggest decision you need to make is whether you will retail your seafood to the end customer or whether you want to wholesale to the retailer. Of course, your profit margins are better if you sell direct to the consumer, but this puts your business into the realm of where you have to be available for hours to wait for customers to show up. With wholesaling, you bring your product to the retailer, drop it off, and you are done.

Perhaps the best of all worlds is to have various routes that you are at for concentrated periods of time. People will get to know that you are in their neck of the woods on Mondays, another place on Tuesdays, and so on. If you are going to set up a truck on the side of the road, you will want to have it there in the late afternoon and catch people on their way home from work. Even if they plan to freeze the seafood they buy and eat it another day, they need to get it to a refrigerator. A good plan might be to have different routes Tuesday through Friday afternoons and early evenings and Saturday mornings.

WHAT YOU WILL NEED

As mentioned above, leased or purchased, one of your most important acquisitions will be a refrigerated truck. This is mandatory for seafood—no iced coolers in the back of a van. You will need an approved accurate scale. Most states have a weights and measures division that oversees the measurement of consumer goods.

You will need a way to wrap the seafood. Typically, fish is wrapped in waxed paper, then wrapped again in wax-lined paper, and taped or banded closed. Other types of seafood, such as scallops, clams, and shrimp, can be bagged in plastic and then double bagged in another larger handled bag.

Handle seafood with plastic gloves designed specifically for food handling. These are inexpensive when bought by the case and should be disposed of each time you handle anything except the seafood.

MARKETING ANGLE

The marketing angle that works best with seafood is FRESH. If you live near the ocean, consumers definitely expect the freshest seafood imaginable. You can be successful selling fresh seafood inland, but you need to prove that your fish is as fresh as can be. If you are within a couple hours' easy flying distance of the ocean, having a relationship with a small-plane owner is critical to fly your product in fresh off the boat. And you will need someone on the other end who is looking out for your interests when purchasing literally off the boat.

NICE TOUCH

Try introducing consumers to new kinds of seafood they may never have tried before. This is where having good recipes can help tremendously. If you are going to introduce people to a new seafood, it is more enticing if you also help them understand how to cook it and what to serve with it. Bring along a portable grill or toaster oven and have something for customers to sample.

EXPANSION POSSIBILITIES

Start small with a few kinds of seafood and expand from there. Especially given the perishable nature of the seafood business, you need to be sure you are responding to customers' wants and selling the seafood you know they will buy. Experiment with adding other items a few at a time and get a sense of whether your customers are interested in squid before loading your truck with squid rings.

WORDS TO KNOW

Calamari: The plural form of the Italian word for squid, *calamaro*.

Farm-raised fish: Fish that is a product of aquacultural production, rather than caught in the wild.

RESOURCES

seafoodbusiness.com: Seafood Business Magazine, the trade magazine for the U.S. seafood industry

solutionsforseafood.com: Conservation Alliance for Seafood Solutions, an alliance of Canadian and U.S. groups that work with businesses and policymakers on seafood management issues.

GOURMET PET FOOD 27

A mericans are spending well over $40 billion a year on our pets. The greatest percentage of that amount is on food. And we show no signs of slowing down in what we will do for Fluffy's and Fido's health and well being. That leaves a lot of room for creating gourmet foods and treats for pets.

You can go the full gourmet pet food shop, especially if your town doesn't have one, or you can make and sell treats to a public eager to show their dogs and cats they love them.

Simply being homemade may be enough of an approach in the animal food and treat arena. Or you can take it the extra mile and go "healthy" or "organic" or "all natural" or whatever tag you think may appeal to the animal lovers in your community.

Dog and cat owners are probably your main targets. Although fish skew the statistics a bit, dogs and cats make up the greater majority of the 252 million pets found in American households. That's a lot of food.

You don't even need to make food: Opening a pet food store where pet owners can shop for only the highest quality foods for their pets would be a very viable option. But decide on the criteria you will use to carry food in your store.

THINGS TO CONSIDER

The big manufacturers have noticed the increasing amounts consumers are willing to spend on their pets, and they have responded accordingly, so pet food a very competitive business. You would do best starting and staying small, perhaps even restricting your business to special treats.

If you make any food or treats to sell, you need to know what kinds of tastes dogs and cats tend to like and particularly things that are either toxic or not good for them, such as onions and chocolate.

HOW DO YOU WANT TO SPEND YOUR DAY?

If you are an animal lover, spending your day creating and working in a shop that caters to the well-being of pets can be a very rewarding way to spend your day. You can even bring your own dog to work with you!

WHAT YOU WILL NEED

Everything about a pet food store can be extremely basic. But if you want to go high-end, you need to look high end. That doesn't mean you have to spend a lot of money but spending money on the right things is important. Your store needs to look high quality, which usually means natural wood and attractive displays.

MARKETING ANGLE

The most important thing to remember when it comes to marketing your pet food business is that your customers are people—not pets! You need to appeal to the pet owner's desire to provide their beloved dog or cat with the very best. That means making sure you angle your marketing to human emotions. Make sure your packaging is appealing and the marketing copy you write or have written is speaking to the human consumer.

NICE TOUCH

One thing that appeals to pet owners more than almost anything is to be able to have their dog accompany them. Invite the pooches in! In fact, have samples for visiting dogs to try the different kinds of food you offer. And if you do decide to make and sell gourmet treats, use broken ones or the end of the batch to break up into smaller pieces and hand out as samples at the checkout counter.

EXPANSION POSSIBILITIES

Expand your shop into a base of pet nutrition knowledge. Conduct classes on feeding dogs and cats. Educate attendees on why the foods you carry are better for pets than the foods found at the dollar store. Talk about other healthy habits, too, such as the importance of exercise. And enlist veterinarians and veterinary technicians to lead workshops and seminars on general health concerns and preventive care. And, of course, offer a small discount on any purchases made by attendees!

WORDS TO KNOW

Antioxidants: Compounds found in certain foods that are known to be cancer-deterring agents. Many pet foods, especially homemade and gourmet foods, now contain antioxidant foods.

Labeling: All pet foods must abide by strict standards when it comes to labeling. If your pet food makes certain health claims, these must be substantiated. Learn what these guidelines are and be sure to follow them.

RESOURCES

catchannel.com
healthrecipes.com

28 NATURAL BABY FOOD

$$

Everyone is concerned about what is in the food they feed their children. With talk of pesticides, growth hormones, and genetically engineered and altered plants and seeds, homemade natural baby food is an appealing idea indeed.

Start with your family and friends and see if making natural baby food is actually an appealing way for you to spend your time. As with beverages, with close attention to all the details, baby food is another business that can grow from a kitchen table business to a business strong enough to sell to a major baby food manufacturer.

There are many possible approaches to the baby food business. One is to simply open up a children's retail shop and carry only brands that fit your mission to present wholesome baby food to the market. Instead of parents having to weed through the grocery store aisle themselves reading labels for the types of food they are seeking, you can pre-select for them and carry only the foods that they are looking for.

You can pick up on parents' own vegetarian leanings. Your natural/homemade baby foods should be relatively sugar-free. Your selection should include cereals and desserts as well as vegetables and meats.

An overall child's retail store can include other "organic" and "natural" baby products such as cotton and wool apparel as well as educational toys, games, and books.

A great approach to making baby food is to continue to follow the trend toward "locally grown" foods. You might consider selling these homemade baby foods at the same farmer's markets where the locally grown produce itself is sold.

THINGS TO CONSIDER

Perhaps the biggest thing to consider when creating baby food products or food for children in general is food allergies. Whatever is in your baby food should be clearly listed in the ingredients list. Parents need to know about any nut products, especially peanuts, to which many children are allergic, some fatally so. Also, many children are allergic to dairy. Keep all of this in mind when you create your products and your labeling.

HOW DO YOU WANT TO SPEND YOUR DAY?

The approach you decide to take will determine what your day in the baby food business will be like. If it's the food-creation element that you are most interested in, then you will want to be making the baby food you plan to sell. If you are most interested in helping parents find high-quality foods for their baby, you can be the middle person doing the pre-screening and offering for sale only the best of what is already out there. Perhaps you were hoping to spend your time working directly with parents and their babies—you might be able to combine both the food-making and the direct contact. Maybe you could hold regular "baby food tastings"!

WHAT YOU WILL NEED

If you are going to make homemade baby foods, the most important things you will need are high-quality ingredients. Next to that, you will need blenders and food processors to mash foods up into edible purees for ease of eating. You'll also need dicers and choppers and a set of high-quality knives to cut food into smaller pieces to make them easier to blend.

You'll need an immaculately clean space to make the food. And you will need some cooking utensils for foods that need cooking, which most foods do if you are going to bottle them. You'll need bottles to put them in and sealed lids. And you'll need basic canning equipment that includes funnels and utensils that make the bottling process easier, as well as cooling racks.

Lastly, you will want to create detailed labels that include your business name, all ingredients, the date when the food was made, and the recommended expiration date.

MARKETING ANGLE

Whenever you put any food item into a container for sale, you need to consider packaging very carefully. This starts with your business name— what you call your baby food business should be appealing to parents who are think about the health of their child.

NICE TOUCH

There is a reason baby food comes in small bottles: Babies don't eat a lot at one sitting. Package your foods in small portions as well. Consider having a "frequency discount," such as buy a dozen jars, get the 13th one free.

EXPANSION POSSIBILITIES

Maybe you decide to get out of the baby-food business—which is time consuming—and simply stock natural foods and other items in a "natural baby" retail store. Also, baby-food customers are lost through natural attrition; babies grow up and eat regular foods. You could package "adult" food into child-friendly packaging and retain some customers that way. If you have a retail outlet, you can gradually begin to expand into other children's related "natural" items and retain your customer base long after the baby has outgrown your food.

WORDS TO KNOW

Additives: Anything from growth hormones fed to the cows that produce the milk we drink, to vitamin and mineral additives, to preservatives used to give food a longer shelf life.

Botulism: A paralytic illness. When ingested by infants, the bacteria in honey make a toxin that can cause infant botulism, a rare and serious form of food poisoning. Infants under 12 months of age should never be fed honey.

RESOURCES

cafemom.com

simplybabyfoodrecipes.com

29 RESTAURANT CLEANING SERVICE

If you offer top-notch service, restaurant cleaning will rarely have "down time." Whether the restaurant had ten customers or a hundred, it is imperative that it is cleaned before the next opening day.

The economy is in a downturn as of this writing, but that doesn't seem to have slowed down the restaurant business much. People need to eat, so when they can't buy the big ticket items such as cars and appliances, they spend money on smaller treats, such as dining out. Any restaurant that's open needs you to clean it!

For general cleaning, you will do the dining area floors and the bathrooms. Bartenders usually clean the bar itself, but leave the floor to the cleaning service. Typically, the restaurant staff takes care of the kitchen area at the end of each work day.

To do this kind of cleaning, you will need to fit in a couple of restaurants pretty early in the day, before they open, or be willing to work late at night.

The other kind of restaurant cleaning work you can try for is the major cleaning that takes place on a day the restaurant is closed. Most restaurants have one, perhaps even two days a week that they are closed; restaurants that rely on business traffic for lunch are often open for dinner only on the weekends, which creates time for major cleaning work.

This more considerable work may include a thorough cleaning of the kitchen areas, including equipment such as fryolators, grills, refrigerators, and freezers. It may also include cleaning things such as ice cream freezers and stock cabinets.

In the dining room, a major cleaning will involve washing windows, bases of tables, and perhaps besides just vacuuming, steam cleaning the rugs. All restaurants are different, and there may be cleaning projects unique to a specific restaurant.

THINGS TO CONSIDER

Depending on how much you want to work and how flexible you want to be, you can take on several restaurants to clean, but you will probably need to have a varied clientele, with some breakfast restaurants and some dinner-only restaurants. If you do any 24-hour restaurants, you will need to do your cleaning while there may be customers in the restaurant.

If you decide to hire people to help you grow your business, be sure they are honest beyond a shadow of a doubt. Most restaurants will be entrusting you with the key to their business and will want to be assured that you and your staff are trustworthy.

Think about how much you want to earn in your cleaning business. Only you can decide if the added work of having employees is worth the additional income you get from being able to take on more clients. It certainly should be in principle, but your personality has a lot to do with whether it is worth having employees or whether you can make enough with the number of clients you can take on yourself.

One way to have employees help you grow is to take on one employee who works with you. Your cleaning jobs will go faster, you will have some company with you while you work (which may be a helpful security factor if you are working late at night), and you will have help if you need to move a big table.

HOW DO YOU WANT TO SPEND YOUR DAY?

Cleaning restaurants is a great job for anyone who loves behind-the-scenes work where you are not required to deal with the public. You will, however, need to have a rapport with restaurant owners to get the work. That said, restaurants will be more interested in your cleaning abilities than your interpersonal skills. If their restaurant always looks immaculate when you are done, you will have job security.

WHAT YOU WILL NEED

You will need all manner of cleaning equipment and supplies. You will need a vacuum cleaner, but most restaurants have central vacuum cleaners where you simply move the hose around from one vacuum connection to another. When taking on the job, be sure to ask if it is your responsibility to empty the vacuum container, which is probably in the basement or a utility closet. Whether it is your responsibility or not, you should make sure someone shows you how to do it so that you can empty it when it fills while you are cleaning.

MARKETING ANGLE

Your best marketing angle is going to be how well you clean restaurants. Get testimonials from your long-term clients. Any cleaning business wants to be known for getting into all the nooks and crannies and going beyond the call of duty to make any restaurant they serve as clean as possible.

There are two major differences between cleaning restaurants and other cleaning jobs:

1. You are creating a clean space where the public will be eating food—their expectations will be very high

2. Restaurants are subject to inspection by the board of health. Any infraction will create bad publicity that a restaurant will have difficulty overcoming.

The other important marketing angle is to promote the fact that you concentrate on restaurant cleaning. Besides the two unique things mentioned above, the restaurant business is subject to very unique cleaning requirements, and your clients will want to be assured you understand this.

NICE TOUCH

The nicest touch you can provide your clients is to do an incredible cleaning job and be undeniably trustworthy.

Another thing you can do for restaurant owners is to keep a checklist of things to alert them about should you run across a problem. These things may be burned out light bulbs, outlets that don't work, trim on tables that is coming unglued. Wait staff often don't notice these things, and many don't remember to tell anyone. If you can leave the owner a checklist of things that need attention, it can help them keep the physical plant running smoothly.

EXPANSION POSSIBILITIES

The most logical way to expand in the restaurant cleaning business is to take on additional restaurants. The only way to do this is to clone yourself—or hire employees. How much you want to deal with employees is a decision only you can make. You can create a larger business and earn more money, but other people are out there representing you. And you are bringing in more money but handing over a portion of it to the employees when you pay their salaries and benefits.

WORDS TO KNOW

Caustic: A substance that may burn exposed skin. Read labels and be careful to wear gloves when using these substances.

Neutralizers: Enzymes that neutralize odors rather than just mask them.

RESOURCES

mycleaningproducts.com: natural cleaning products

wholesalejanitorialsupply.com

FOOD COOPERATIVE   30

A food cooperative is a great way to buy high-quality food products at good prices, using the benefits of ordering in quantity. Food co-ops are often non-profits, and the contemporary concept is a holdover from the hippie era, but it doesn't have to be this way. Connoisseurs can use the idea to be able to buy anything from caviar to truffles. Great things that can be bought as a co-op include high-quality olive oil, seafood, and other high-priced items.

If you want your co-op to include wine purchases, you need to carefully check your state's liquor laws. There can be ways around this, such as "supper clubs," for instance, whose diners are members, and the clubs don't fall under the usual liquor laws.

You aren't going to make huge money with a food co-op concept. If you were looking for that, you might as well open a regular grocery store (although even grocery stores don't make huge profits, but they are great revenue generators).

How does a co-op work? The main beauty of a co-op is the fact that everything is purchased per order of the members. You can require money up front to cover the cost of purchasing and to be sure that no one leaves you high and dry by never picking up (or paying for) what they ordered.

You can make your money by adding a percentage to the costs that you are quoted for what you are ordering (which might be hard to do unless you know how much you will be ordering). Or you can require membership fees. Or both.

One of your jobs might be to look for good deals on interesting foods in which the co-op members might be interested. If you maintain an e-mail list (which you should), you can e-mail everyone about something you find and test the interest. If the members express sufficient interest, you can ask them to place an order.

THINGS TO CONSIDER

One way you might be able to capitalize on unexpected things you find is to have members set up a prepaid account with the co-op. This doesn't mean you can use the account without their order, but if you e-mail members with a good deal and they want to be part of an order, you don't have to collect all sorts of separate credit card payments; you can just make the purchase and deduct each member's share from their prepaid account (with their permission).

You will want to have regular meetings—no more than quarterly or even every six months—to discuss ideas and get member feedback on how the co-op is operating and what kinds of items they would like you to offer.

HOW DO YOU WANT TO SPEND YOUR DAY?

Running a food co-op is sort of like being paid to shop for people. That's the fun part! You also will need to unpack things that come in, split them into the appropriate orders, and prepare the orders for pick up.

You should plan to spend your Saturdays loading member's orders. You will need to decide if you can offer a second pickup time, since some people won't be able to make it on Saturdays. You can also decide to open the co-op to the public on Saturdays and sell any overage you ordered, which can also be a way to make extra money. If you are not set up as a nonprofit, this extra money does not have to go to the membership—that's a key difference. This is your business, based on a co-op model.

WHAT YOU WILL NEED

You will need a modest storefront. The good news is not only does it not need to be in a high-cost retail area, it is better if it is not. One of those out-of-town (but still safe) strip malls is perfect—the spaces are usually wide open, or at least easy to renovate, for you to do whatever you want. Each storefront usually has three or four parking spaces right in front of the store so members can back right up to the door to load their orders.

You will need shelving to be able to arrange orders. Get a supply of sturdy cardboard boxes and canvas tote bags and require members to either bring them back to load their next order or they will be charged to get new ones.

You will also need some refrigeration and freezer space if you plan to get perishables.

MARKETING ANGLE

For those who are reluctant to join in on the co-op idea, create a trial membership and let people try the idea out. The biggest marketing angle you will need to get people interested is that using your co-op is easy. Be sure to have an online presence and do lots via e-mail.

NICE TOUCH

Co-ops tend to be environmentally responsible. Provide your co-op members with reusable canvas totes to bring home their orders. The totes also are great publicity to get potential members interested.

EXPANSION POSSIBILITIES

One way to expand your co-op idea is to set up co-ops in other areas not too far from you. You will need to hire someone to help staff that satellite store, especially on Saturdays or whenever you arrange to have pickup times.

WORDS TO KNOW

Board of Directors: Membership-based organizations have a board of directors who are elected by the membership and oversee the overall operation of the organization.

Membership: Most co-ops operate on a membership basis, which may or may not include dues.

RESOURCES

olympiafood.coop: an example of a food cooperative in the northwest

putneycoop.com: an example of a food cooperative in the northeast

ICE CREAM STAND 31

Ice cream is so popular, it is practically a food group all its own. That makes it a great potential business.

You would, however, be opening a mini-restaurant of sorts, which presents its own unique set of issues to consider. People are very demanding about their food, as is the board of health about food service places. The informality of an ice cream shop does not mean you can be informal about how you handle the details of food service. But all of that aside, an ice cream business can be fun and financially rewarding.

You can either open an honest-to-goodness stationary ice cream stand or you can set up a rolling freezer to sell ice cream on the sidewalk. And you can choose to make your own ice cream, or you can find an ice cream manufacturer whose product you like (that will be a fun taste-testing experience!) to sell at your stand. Ice cream manufacturers usually require exclusivity, so keep that in mind as you are testing. That exclusivity, however, gives you a little leverage when it comes to getting some marketing dollars.

The key here, especially given the $5,000 limitation, is to start small. There are many things you can do for future expansion, as is outlined below, but in the beginning focus on ice cream, ice cream, ice cream. You might even forego the other ice cream treats such as sundaes and milkshakes and truly focus just on serving up a perfect ice cream cone. That said, you will want a variety of flavors and perhaps some nuts or candy sprinkles to go on top. But in the beginning, you don't need to get more complicated than that.

THINGS TO CONSIDER

Despite ice cream's popularity, you can't get too confident, because such a popular food has a lot of competition. Almost everything under the sun to distinguish an ice cream business has been tried. The important thing is to sell excellent ice cream—whether you make it yourself on the premises or buy it from a high-quality ice cream maker doesn't matter as long as it is delicious.

Also, ice cream vendors seem to think that they need to provide giant portions to keep people happy. Certainly, you should offer a super size for those big eaters. But most people can't even eat a huge portion of ice cream before it is almost melted, which is especially frustrating when it is on a cone. If you are one who thinks that you should provide a huge ice cream serving so you can charge a premium price, think again. Pricing is one of the greatest competing elements when you are up against other ice cream vendors with an excellent product. Create reasonable portions at reasonable prices in varying sizes to meet all appetites, and you will have lines out your door.

HOW DO YOU WANT TO SPEND YOUR DAY?

This is a business where you will most likely want to have a few employees. You probably won't want to be spend most of your waking hours dipping ice cream, but this is a great job for someone in high school.

You will be dealing with the public. And when it comes to what goes in their stomachs, the public can be something to deal with. If you start small, keep your business immaculately clean, and sell premium ice cream at reasonable prices, you will make the public happy.

WHAT YOU WILL NEED

If you keep your ice cream stand simple to start, your needs can be kept to a minimum. The most important thing, of course, is to offer the most delicious ice cream in the area.

The other thing you will need is a great location. You need to be in a place where getting an ice cream cone makes sense. Where your location is will be very specific to your area. If you can find a great independent spot along a busy road that has a safe place for people to pull off and park, that might work. Or you can check out the strip malls and become a destination point. Being "in town" is going to be expensive as far as rent goes, and the chances are slim that there is not already an ice cream location there.

Whatever you choose for a location, the fitting out of your shop can be very simple. The most important things you will need are a couple of large chest freezers to hold the tubs of ice cream. And you will need another freezer or two in a back room to store extra tubs of ice cream. Leasing a location that already has a walk-in freezer would be ideal but at first, you don't need to store that much back inventory, so while convenient, it is far from necessary.

Then, of course, you will need the ice cream. It will take you some time to learn how to order for your shop, so start off conservatively. Chances are you will be getting your ice cream from a manufacturer who can supply you pretty quickly if you run out.

Whether you make your own ice cream or sell someone else's is up to you. Of course, making your own ice cream is ideal, but there are so many high-quality products on the market you don't need to make it yourself in order to sell good ice cream. It depends on what your goals are.

To make your own ice cream, you will need a commercial ice cream maker; noncommercial models just don't make enough quantity. You can buy these used and stay within your price range for startup. Making your own ice cream also requires that you have adequate space to do it, usually behind the scenes and sometimes off premises.

You will need containers to hold the ice cream you make; five-gallon tubs are typical. You will want plenty of ice cream scoops! They are like pens in their ability to disappear. And you will need cones of different varieties, paper cups to sell ice cream in bowls, spoons, and a huge supply of napkins.

And then you need customers! Getting people to an ice cream stand is often just as easy as getting bees to honey—but customers need a great experience to keep them coming back.

MARKETING ANGLE

Your best marketing angle is going to depend on the ice cream competition in your market area. If there are several other delicious ice cream vendors within a two- or three-mile radius, you will need something else besides delicious ice cream to stand out.

You can also have some fun and sponsor a few contests such as ice cream eating or scooping contests. Do some charity fundraisers with this kind of contest and become known in your area as a business that supports local charities or people in need.

NICE TOUCH

If you have a lot of competition, add a frequent buyer card to your marketing scheme. After customers have bought ten cones, they get the eleventh for free, or something of that sort.

Set up a board that allows you to slide names of ice cream in and out. That way you don't have to be out of anything; it can just be removed from the board when you are out of it. Be sure to put the name back up when inventory is back, or you may discover that no one is ordering the chocolate chip supreme because no one knows about it! But having a flavor removed from the board is better than disappointing customers who are looking forward to a flavor only to get to the front of the line and find out you don't have it. And it's better than having names of ice creams crossed off a list, which looks like you don't know how to keep inventory.

If you make your own ice cream, being out of flavors might be more acceptable. But these days, people expect to have everything all the time, so it is best to make them continue to think that they can.

EXPANSION POSSIBILITIES

Of course, the greatest expansion possibility with ice cream is adding other food items to the menu. Once you are into any kind of food, this is the logical thing to do. However, you need to establish yourself as the best ice cream vendor in the area before diluting your offering with other types of foods. So before you add hot dogs and hamburgers and other sandwiches, chips, fries, or whatever, start by adding other ice cream dishes such as sundaes and milkshakes if you didn't start out that way.

WORDS TO KNOW

Gelatin: An ingredient often added to ice cream to stabilize it.
Hand crank: Before the advent of electric machines, ice cream was made in a hand-cranked mixer.

RESOURCES

makeicecream.com: White Mountain Ice Cream Makers, sellers of used commercial ice cream making supplies
cartsandgrills.com

32 SUBSCRIPTION GARDEN

$$

A subscription garden, also known as Community-Supported Agriculture (CSA), is when people sign up in advance to be regularly supplied with what you harvest from your garden. There are many ways to do it. You can have subscribers tell you what they would like you to provide them with. Or, especially to start, you can grow what you think you have the room, the right soil, and the right area for and provide your subscribers with regular deliveries of a specified quantity of whatever is in season.

So in late June, you may show up with a basket full of the fastest-growing early vegetables such as lettuces, radishes, spinach, peas, summer squash, and strawberries. By late July, the basket may contain tomatoes, peppers, and cucumbers. And in the fall, you will be delivering winter squashes, pumpkins, and other hardy and long-growing produce.

After you have done your subscription garden for a couple years, you can begin to ask customers what they want for produce (if they haven't told you already) and grow a more custom product, unless your garden isn't suitable for what they want.

THINGS TO CONSIDER

Don't promise your subscribers anything. Growing food is fraught with potential problems—insect infestations, a season of weather not conducive to a particular crop—so you don't want to promise anything you can't deliver. Tell them what you are growing this season. Make it clear you offer no guarantees about what actually makes it from planting to harvesting. Of course, if very little is harvested or every year you have no corn even though you planted an acre of it, then you need to adjust your gardening practices!

HOW DO YOU WANT TO SPEND YOUR DAY?

Growing a commercial-sized garden is hard physical work. It is also incredibly enjoyable for those who like to till the soil and do garden work.

And you may think gardening is just a one-season business, but in reality, there are only a couple of months, even in the north, when you will be doing no gardening-related work. Perhaps you can take December and January off, but in February and March, you will need to spend time poring over the seed catalogs that will pile into your mailbox. You will also need to use that time to plan your garden: Look through last year's records (and be sure to keep them!) to decide what parts of the plot to rotate with a different crop, what didn't do well in a certain area, and so on.

By late March and definitely April, you will be planting seeds in pots for transplanting; those will need to be watered and, unless you have a greenhouse, they will need to be turned depending on your growing lights. In April and May, you will be preparing the garden itself. May is the planting month in most parts of the country. Of course, the summer months will be busy with continuous plantings of different vegetables and keeping the weeds and pests at bay. At least by late June and throughout the rest of the summer, you will be harvesting and delivering produce! By October, when in the north the chance of frost is getting high, your harvesting and deliveries will slow down but you prepare the garden for the winter and plant things such as garlic and any cover crop. Then, whew, it's December and time for a break!

WHAT YOU WILL NEED

You will need some land to grow your produce. You don't have to own all the land you need; find a place where you might be able to lease an acre or so, depending on what you want to grow and how many subscribers you want to have.

You will need to have gardening tools. Depending on how big your garden gets, you will want to think about a tractor; but tractors are incredibly expensive and even used ones will exceed your $5,000 startup budget several times over. You can rent a tractor for a weekend, which can work perfectly if you condense your tractor-related work to make the best use of the rental time. You should either plan to purchase a power rototiller or hire someone to do that work for you.

Mostly, though, you will need small hand tools that aren't very expensive—but you should still plan to buy the highest quality tools you can find. They will last longer, feel better in your hands, and not tire you so fast. Take excellent care of them, washing them off after each use and never leaving them outside, especially in the rain.

The kind of tools you need include a few different kinds of rakes, a couple of hoes, and a few different kinds of shovels. You may want to own some fencing tools, because deer and woodchucks will be interested in checking out your garden.

You will find some tools along the way that you especially like—different things that help plant seeds, for instance. And there are some other garden structures you will need to buy or make to trellis vine plants such as cucumbers and beans and cages to help tomato plants stand upright under the weight of their ripening fruit.

You will also need a fuel-efficient, reliable vehicle to make your deliveries, which is presumably the vehicle you already own. You can also encourage people to pick up their own weekly subscriptions with a discount incentive, which is an especially good idea if you have added a farmstand and there may be additional sales opportunities.

A basic computer system is a good thing to have as well. You can make your own order lists, send an e-mail newsletter, print row markers, order seeds, even map out your garden with a design program.

MARKETING ANGLE

This is another business where the interest in locally grown food and knowing where your food comes from and how it was grown is the key to customers. Promote this aspect in your marketing materials. If you refrain from using pesticides or chemical fertilizers, be sure to tell people that. Those for whom it doesn't matter will be your customers either way. But for those who do care about pesticide use on their foods, they will not be your customers unless they know this about your produce.

NICE TOUCH

Each year, try a new and unusual vegetable. Provide your subscribers with a recipe or two to help them learn how to cook with these vegetable. Survey them at the end of the season and ask whether they would like to see this vegetable again next year.

Another nice touch is to grow a small plot of flowers and add a small bouquet to each order you deliver.

EXPANSION POSSIBILITIES

Taking on more customers is the obvious way to expand. But in order to do that, you will need more vegetables. In order to grow more vegetables, you will most likely need more space. Ultimately, you will only be able to expand in this business to the extent that you have the time to work your gardens. It would be counterproductive to plant more than you can manage and lose customers because you provide them with lesser quality produce.

You can also expand by having some commercial subscribers, such as restaurants or small markets. Find out what they might specifically like to offer their customers and become their provider of that particular vegetable.

Another great way to expand is to build a simple greenhouse. You can get a jump on the growing season and you might be able to use it for retail space, too, depending on where the greenhouse is located.

Another way to use your greenhouse is to grow seedlings to sell to people to plant in their own gardens. Offer them at a discount to your subscribers—you'd be surprised how many people want to grow a few vegetables of their own but will still subscribe to your garden to get all the things they don't grow themselves.

WORDS TO KNOW

Organic: To be able to call your produce "organic," you need to go through a rigorous and expensive certification process. If this is important to you and your potential subscriber base, by all means find out what this process is in your state. You will need to pass those costs along to your customers, so it pays to check with them to see if it is worth it. You may find that you can build a strong enough relationship with your subscribers that they trust that you are using organic processes even if your farm is not officially certified.

RESOURCES

garden.org: National Gardening Association

organicgardening.com: *Organic Gardening* magazine

pumpkinridgegardens.com: a subscription garden based in Oregon

RECIPE TESTER

33

What fun it can be to be a recipe tester! Most cookbook authors and cooking magazines that provide recipes need to have cooks test the recipes they create and/or publish. You can be one of the several people who help. They will want to know

- if the ingredients are hard to find or hard to work with
- if the recipe is easy to follow
- if the directions are clear
- if all of the steps are included
- if you see or suspect any mistakes in the recipe
- if a tip or two should be added, such a using a special tool
- if the final results meet expectations in taste and appearance.

Recipe testing is not a career you can expect to launch without some skill as a chef. You either need to have some appropriate credentials or you need to plan to get them. An associate's degree or some sort of certificate from a well-respected cooking school is a good start. Having spent time as a chef in a variety of restaurants is also good for your resume. Perhaps you worked for a caterer for many years, or perhaps you are carrying on a family tradition of foodies. Whatever, you do need to have something on your resume that points to your skill as a chef and the ability to follow a complex recipe. And it has to be more than the fact that your kids love your brownies.

You will want to work up a very professional resume to get work in recipe testing. Some of the big publishers of cookbooks and cooking magazines have their own test kitchens, but that doesn't mean they don't hire freelancers as well. Go to cooking trade shows, both local and national, to seek out potential clients. If you live in an area where there is a high concentration of restaurants, perhaps you could gain a client or two testing recipes for a restaurant to try.

Other clients might include cookware manufacturers. Many of them include recipes for use with their products. If you think out of the box and really look around, there are hundreds of possibilities for someone to pick up recipe- and cooking-related work. People have to eat!

THINGS TO CONSIDER

You line up a great job testing recipes in a cookbook manuscript that's in creation for a publisher. The cookbook author just loves you and appreciates your work and the publisher is so glad to have found you. They have a dozens of other cookbook projects coming up and they want you to work on them all. Beware! Don't run out and purchase all the ingredients and special equipment you need for the dozens of cookbooks coming your way. Things have a way of falling apart—editors leave, cookbook authors decide they want to take a break; the list of what can go wrong is endless. Buy the stuff you need to add to your kitchen to do the jobs you have but don't go into debt or end up with machines and gadgets you would otherwise never use until you have the project in hand.

Also, never hesitate to ask if the publisher or author can provide the main ingredients for a particular testing project. Needless to say, they expect you to have a professional oven without their having to buy it (and if you are good at recipe testing, it means you have experience, which means you probably wouldn't dream of cooking without the best oven you can afford). But for things that are very specific to the project they are asking you to test, you can certainly ask for their contribution.

HOW DO YOU WANT TO SPEND YOUR DAY?

Unless you are working on barbecue or grilling projects, this is an indoor job. You will also be on your feet a lot. The upside is that although you will need to work under imposed deadlines, you can pretty much be in control of your day. You can do this work in the evening if you want—you might want to record your favorite TV show to relax over after you have finished the recipe instead of setting up a TV in the kitchen since you will want your testing to have your undivided attention. It only takes an extra teaspoon of baking powder to make a recipe a disaster!

WHAT YOU WILL NEED

To be a recipe tester, you should plan to have a well-appointed professional kitchen. The temperature of your oven needs to be accurate. And your stovetop should provide even heat with a variety of burners.

From there, you will need a collection of utensils and cookware to suit the kinds of recipes you will be testing. Purchase the basics—mixing bowls, measuring spoons, several measuring cups, spatulas, cookie sheets, muffin tins, and loaf pans. Be sure to have sealed containers for flour, sugar, and other perishables. But you don't need to buy everything at once—you can wait to find out if you need a special pan for a particular recipe before purchasing it. That way, you can gradually add to your collection.

MARKETING ANGLE

Your main marketing angle will be your expertise as a cook. If you do have a professionally appointed kitchen, be sure to mention that: You are a turnkey operation ready to help with recipe testing. Also, if you happen to have a specific expertise, such as grilling, baking, handmade pasta, or you are a genius with an omelet pan, be sure that is loud and clear on your resume. Not only might that get you some attention but if you are being considered for a cookbook, knowing this kind of information may put you on an author's radar screen for another book they are working on.

NICE TOUCH

The nicest touch you can do as a recipe tester is to test the recipe more than once and guarantee your accuracy. You could even always test recipes with a few of your friends if you can get enough ingredients from the company for whom you are testing.

EXPANSION POSSIBILITIES

One way to expand is to begin to create recipes as well as test them. Also, cooking classes are a natural extension of recipe testing. You will have begun to develop a professional kitchen—is it expansive enough to hold a small class? If not, you could look around to see if there is a professional kitchen that you could lease on an as-needed basis to conduct classes. You could also offer your services as an assistant to a well-established cookbook author with a cooking show.

WORDS TO KNOW

Blanching: To scald or parboil

Vegan: a vegetarian who eats no animal products whatsoever, including dairy, and often does not use animal products, such as leather.

RESOURCES

americastestkitchen.com

elementsoftaste.com

SPECIALTY DIET CHEF 34

For a chef, this kind of specialty cooking can be among the most rewarding work you do. It is similar to a personal chef business, only you will probably have several clients and the fundamentals of your job will be bit more complex.

Cancer patients—especially those who have undergone chemotherapy—can have great difficulty eating. Nothing tastes great, food certainly tastes different than it did before chemo, and yet patients need to eat in order to regain strength and help their body fight the cancer, as well as the effects of chemotherapy and other treatments. And eating good nutritional food helps cancer patients begin to feel like they are getting back to their pre-cancer lives.

Other chronic diseases also improve when managed with nutritional support: Heart disease, diabetes, high blood pressure, and other conditions require that patients pay close attention to, and probably change, their diets. You can help with both the immediate changes and with adherence to long-term dietary habits. Help with grocery shopping, meal preparation, and overall food choices—even how to eat healthfully in restaurants—can all be part of this business.

You will need some credentials for this field of work. If you have a degree in some kind of nutritional science, that is great. Being a full-fledged registered dietitian probably isn't necessary, but a good way to do this work is to team up with a dietitian who can help you design appropriate recipes and menus.

You can set up a general plan of how to work with people with chronic illnesses, but you definitely need to be flexible. The best way to work with one person may not be the best for another.

A scenario might be to meet with patients in the hospital before they are discharged and talk with them, with a nurse, doctor, and/or hospital dietitian present, to learn about the kinds of food they should eat or should avoid given their individual medical conditions. Talk about what the patients like to eat—even things they are not supposed to eat—so that you can get a sense of what they like.

When the patient is discharged, meet with them in their home to map out the specifics of how you will work: Will you cook in the patient's home? Cook meals ahead of time and freeze them? Cook for just the patient or the entire family? What kind of freezer do they have? If you are to cook in the home, how is their kitchen equipped? Is there anything you need, a small appliance or particular utensil? Will you be teaching the patient or a member of the patient's family to cook for the patient? This is a complicated business, but it can be very rewarding.

THINGS TO CONSIDER

This business requires you to be more than just a foodie. This is serious medical business. You need to be aware that cancer treatment is a roller coaster—your client may be upbeat and eager to work with you one week and not care that you are there the next. You can't be too sensitive about your food creations—no matter how good something tastes to you, the chemicals involved in chemotherapy do crazy things to taste buds. And the effect of the disease itself—just feeling sick and weak— can make food just seem unappealing. Other medical conditions may not wreak as much havoc on the patient's sense of taste, but they can add to whether the person can muster the ability to care about eating habits or eating at all.

This is where you will need to be a bit of a coach and be creative in your food preparation. Perhaps playing on a person's sense of not wanting to hurt your feelings can be a way to help them eat at least a small portion of what your prepare. This isn't about your food, even though the benefits of eating well are fairly well documented. It is hard to force someone to do something they really don't want to do.

You also want to think beyond the obvious—find out if there is some underlying issue, such as medication that leaves sores in the mouth or tooth sensitivity, that makes some foods difficult to eat.

HOW DO YOU WANT TO SPEND YOUR DAY?

Your days will mostly be spent researching foods that might be helpful to a patient and creating menus and perhaps even recipes. You will want to consult regularly with your dietitian colleague. And you need to be willing to spend time with people who are perhaps on the mend but still are sick and not necessarily themselves.

WHAT YOU WILL NEED

You should plan to have a computer to do research on foods and recipes. Also, plan to learn as much as possible about the conditions of the people for whom you will be cooking. Be sure to limit your research to extremely reliable sites, such as the American Medical Association, the Mayo Clinic, the Cleveland Clinic, and other well-known medical websites. You can, however, tap into e-mail groups that are focused on a specific condition— you may learn a lot about how people cope with the condition and what they are experiencing as far as eating goes.

MARKETING ANGLE

The tricky thing here is figuring out who will pay you. Most cancer patients and others with chronic conditions don't usually have the resources to hire a personal chef while they are sick. In fact, financial difficulty is problematic with major medical issues, even when the person has health insurance: They often can't work, short-term disability is expensive, and long-term disability insurance doesn't kick in for several months. Few, if any, health insurance policies cover nutritional care during medical treatments of any kind.

So to whom do you market yourself? One way to approach this kind of work is to establish a relationship with a medical center. Focusing on cancer can be one aspect, but any major medical problem can be a target for nutritional support. Heart disease, high blood pressure, and diabetes are certainly chronic health problems that need nutritional attention.

NICE TOUCH

Learn a lot about cooking with herbs and finding ways to make meals flavorful for those who may not feel like eating. Also, many conditions require low salt intake—herbs and spices can go a long way to make up for the seasoning that salt usually provides.

EXPANSION POSSIBILITIES

There are a couple of ways to expand this business. You could offer classes for patients or family members in how to prepare menus for the specific condition they have. These classes will need to be conducted by disease condition since each one has such different requirements. Alternatively, or in conjunction with classes, you could do a newsletter with information and recipes. Make your newsletter an e-mail one so you don't need to spend money printing it. Or, if you do print it, try to distribute it in hospitals and doctor's offices. You could also do prepared meals and sell them on a subscription basis. Your first task, however, is to gain credibility among the medical community in order to gain credibility with potential clients.

WORDS TO KNOW

Diabetes: A hormonal disorder that involves the body's ability to produce or properly use insulin. Diabetes requires strict dietary monitoring to regulate, typically along with medication or insulin injections.

Food pyramid: The USDA chart that shows the recommended daily intake for each of the five food groups.

RESOURCES

eatright.org, The American Dietetic Association is the licensing organization for registered dietitians and can provide a list of R.D.s in your area.

jameshaller.com, a website from someone who cooks for people with chronic health problems

35 PICK-YOUR-OWN FARM

If you have the space, a pick-your-own fruit farm might be just the thing! This can be a highly successful agribusiness. If you live outside a population center, which you probably do if you own farmland, that doesn't mean you can't have a thriving operation. But you will need to work a little harder to create an attractive destination so potential customers make the effort to travel to the hinterlands to your farm.

But first, the basics. Unless you want to be open just during a concentrated time period, you will want to have a variety of fruits and vegetables to keep your customers coming back throughout the year.

For instance, you could have

- a mix of berries that start fairly early in the season, from strawberries to raspberries, blackberries, blueberries, and elderberries
- fruit trees, including different varieties of pears, peaches, quince, apples, and even citrus fruits
- an endless array of salad vegetables: peppers, tomatoes, cucumbers, greens, onions, carrots, radishes, and so on
- herbs such as basil, oregano, different kinds of parsley, and garlic
- root vegetables such as winter, acorn, and butternut squash
- other vegetables such as summer squashes, asparagus, broccoli, Brussels sprouts, and cabbage
- cut flowers from cosmos to zinnias and especially sunflowers
- pumpkins and gourds in a variety of types and sizes
- Christmas trees, wreaths, kissing balls, and greens for decorating.

A lot of what you offer will depend on the amount and type of land you have. With farming and gardening of any kind, a lot of things suddenly need to happen at once—watering, weeding, pruning, pest control, harvesting. The bigger you get, the more help you will need to keep everything thriving. People who come to your farm expect the highest quality produce.

THINGS TO CONSIDER

The pick-your-own aspect, like almost everything, has its upsides and its downsides. Having customers pick their own fruit can be a great marketing approach to your business—it gives people a real sense of accomplishment, and it is a great family activity. On the other hand, you will have people out in your fruit orchards. You need to give very specific directions about picking.

Consider providing a small instruction sheet—perhaps even something that is laminated and attached to gathering baskets—in order to help remind them how to consider fruit ripe and how to pick without harming the plant or tree. Be sure your rows are very clearly defined so that people know where to walk and don't trample berry bushes. And even though it is a great family activity, parents need to know to keep their children under their direction at all times.

HOW DO YOU WANT TO SPEND YOUR DAY?

A PYO farm can be the best of both worlds. You will deal with the public for sure, but you also need to tend to your crops. So you can be on your own pruning fruit trees, fertilizing berry bushes, and just generally checking on your crops. Or you can be assisting customers, helping them get going and directing them to the day's picking area and cashing out their fruits and berries.

WHAT YOU WILL NEED

You will need land. To stay within the $5,000 startup parameters, you will probably need to own the land already. If not, you can search for land to lease or that you can buy at a reasonable price. A couple of acres of good, arable land can be the seed property for a larger operation.

You will need seeds, plants, canes, saplings, or whatever is appropriate for what crops you want to start with for your PYO venture. A few basic tools should be sufficient to get things planted and to tend to your crop after it is in the ground. Eventually, you will definitely want your own tractor, but in the beginning, you can hire someone with a tractor or rent a tractor for a weekend to do the big projects.

Keep the customer in mind when you are planning your garden beds and layout. You want them to be able to get to the fruits and vegetables easily enough without trampling everything around them. You will want everything nicely spaced and clearly marked.

Besides having customers pick their own produce, you can also harvest a certain amount for those customers who want fresh fruits and vegetables but don't want to pick their own. Or perhaps they'd like to pick blueberries with their kids, but also would pick up a basketful of fresh vegetables while they are there. For that, you will want some kind of simple farmstand.

Depending on what you have for crops, you will need support framework. This can range from sticks and string to tomato cages and other things that are specific to the particular crops you are selling.

MARKETING ANGLE

The marketing angle you should emphasize is the concept of fresh food raised locally with safe, trusted methods by local farmers. This is the wave of the future: Knowing where your food is from. It is a compelling marketing angle. Do your research and find the information you need to convince people that this is the way to go in buying their food.

NICE TOUCH

A nice touch is to carry your "locally grown" and "environmentally friendly" message completely through your business. Have canvas and paper bags available, and use cardboard boxes. Use natural pest control, solar lighting and electric fencing if you need to keep out animals such as woodchucks and deer. Give the appearance inside and out that customers can be confident of your environmental approach.

EXPANSION POSSIBILITIES

Expansion possibilities will revolve around the idea of making your PYO farm a destination for customers, so they will want to bring the family and stay a while. Perhaps have tables where they can enjoy a picnic, or maybe have sandwiches and drinks for sale. Add a small petting zoo for kids—and their parents—to learn about sheep and wool, or goat's milk, or chickens and eggs. Corn mazes are popular; even a small one can be an attraction. Hiring someone to give horse drawn hay rides or sleigh rides in winter can be a nice addition to pumpkin harvesting or Christmas tree sales.

WORDS TO KNOW

PYO: Short for "pick your own," these kinds of farms are also called "U-pick" or "cut your own" for Christmas trees.

Corn maze: a walking maze made out of the remains of a cornfield; often added to ag businesses to make the business a destination point

RESOURCES

foodshedalliance.org

littlewoodfarm.org

$$$

36 FARM-RAISED, FREE-RANGE MEAT

Consumers not only want to know more about the source of their fruits, vegetables, and milk, they are also willing to pay a premium to be more knowledgeable about how and where their meat is raised. With growth hormones and chemical feed additives becoming more and more controversial, many consumers feel it's time to be more proactive about seeking out meat raised by local farmers. Here's where you can come in.

Raising cattle, chickens, and pigs on a small scale to sell locally might not be a big moneymaking venture, but it can pay for itself and cover the cost of your own meat in the process. If you can get some restaurant customers, you can, in fact, make some money at it.

The USDA offers no regulatory definition of the term "free range" beyond the fact that in order for chicken to be labeled as "free-range" raised, the birds needed to have access to the outdoors while raised for meat. Free-range in general refers to animals being able to live normal lives for their species. Chickens are allowed to roam around and eat bugs and peck in the dirt. Pigs can wallow in mud holes and root up stumps. Cattle are not confined to a feedlot to wait until they weigh enough to make them profitable and, in the case of veal, young calves are not confined to small pens. They have room to roam and graze according to the norms of their species and interact with each other as a herd or flock.

This is not typically how our meat is grown on a commercial scale. Chickens live in quarters so confined they almost can't move. Their beaks are clipped so they don't peck at each other. Turkeys are confined and fed so much to make them the huge birds that people have come to expect for their Thanksgiving meal, that the turkey's legs eventually can't support its own weight; the bird can't move at all for the last portion of its short life.

These are the conditions that "free-range" looks to avoid. And if you are careful to market your meat with this information, the growing number of people who desire this kind of husbandry will seek out your homegrown, free-range meat.

THINGS TO CONSIDER

Whether you call it free range or not, no matter how you raise your animals, if you plan to sell their meat, you need to be comfortable with raising animals for meat—you can't consider them as pets. You don't have to slaughter them yourself; in fact, food regulations do not allow you to do that without setting up an expensive processing area. However, you need to emotionally be able to load them on the truck to go to the slaughterhouse. Some people can do this without any hesitation, others can't. If you are one of the former, you can be a great source of meat for people who want to know that the animals that are giving their lives to become food at least had good lives of their own while they were on the planet.

HOW DO YOU WANT TO SPEND YOUR DAY?

You will spend your day tending to animals. If you are not feeding, you will be cleaning their pens. If you are not cleaning their pens, you will be doctoring the animals when they develop problems, which they do no matter how carefully you take care of them. If you aren't doctoring them yourself, you will be waiting for the veterinarian to come. You also need to make sure there is adequate and appropriate food and bedding. And as anyone who has kept farm animals will tell you, when you think there is nothing else to do, there is always fence mending and construction!

WHAT YOU WILL NEED

You will need to already have an appropriate property to raise the animals you choose to raise. This will differ greatly, as you might imagine, depending on what type of animals you decide to market. Chickens and rabbits, which require minimal space to be happy, are on one side of the spectrum while cattle, which require a lot of space, are on the other.

If you don't already own property, another option is to try to lease some land. Keep in mind, however, that you will be installing fencing and constructing housing that will benefit the landowner, not you. Perhaps you can arrange the lease to reduce the lease payments by a percentage of the housing and fencing if you leave it behind when the lease ends.

Fencing needs will range from not much to heavy duty—although for most small livestock such as chickens, ducks, geese, and rabbits, the fencing is primarily to keep predators out, not to keep the animals in.

MARKETING ANGLE

Although you will spend most of your time tending to the animals themselves and their peripheral needs, such as housing and fencing, you will also need to spend time on marketing or hire someone else to do it. Your main angle is, of course, the free-range aspect of your operation. There are many people who want to feel better about eating meat by at least knowing that the animals enjoyed life and were slaughtered in the quickest and most humane way possible.

The other marketing angle is the people who buy their meat from you as opposed to the grocery store, know where the meat is raised and whether or not you use growth hormones (probably not, because using such drugs would be counter to your free-range approach) and other things such as medicated feeds.

To market your meat products, consider creating meat packages. Offer different packages for all sizes of families. You can sell an entire dressed hog in varying cuts, or a side of beef and its different cuts, or mix and match with pork, beef, chicken, perhaps a turkey, and a couple of more exotic choices, such as rabbit stew meat and buffalo burger.

In a business like this, your marketing materials should reflect the wholesome, natural approach you are taking with your products.

NICE TOUCH

As with any "raw" food business of this kind, it is always a nice touch to include some recipes with your meat packages. At the very least, be sure customers know how to cook any of the more unusual cuts, such as rabbit or buffalo.

EXPANSION POSSIBILITIES

Starting simple in a labor-intensive business such as one that involves raising live animals is always a wise approach. Perhaps you get your homegrown, free-range meat business started with chickens and a few hogs. Expansion for you could simply mean that once you are experienced with one type of animal, you add another.

If your setup is right, you could add a small roadside stand to your operation. You will, however, need to have some refrigeration and electricity access to showcase at least some portion of your offerings.

Another expansion possibility in this market is to add upper-scale restaurants and/or specialty markets to your customer base. This kind of expansion means you would be selling your meat at wholesale prices. It would also mean an increase in the amount of meat you sell, but that increase would mean increasing your overhead in the number of animals you raise.

WORDS TO KNOW

Pastured poultry: Chickens and turkeys raised on pasture rather than in confinement.

Stocking density: The number of animals in a certain amount of area. It is not necessarily equivalent to free range.

RESOURCES

apppa.org: American Pastured Poultry Producers Association

cowboyfreerangemeat.com: Cowboy Free Range Meat

HOMEMADE SALSA

37

S alsa has nearly surpassed ketchup as the favored condiment in the United States. Typically a no-fat, no-sugar food, traditional salsa is easy to make and easy to vary, so you can be creative with it.

Salsa's main ingredients are tomatoes, peppers, onions, and, typically, cilantro. After a lot of chopping, you have a great dip for chips or sauce for fish, eggs, or whatever else you feel like slathering it on!

You don't have to grow your own tomatoes, peppers, and onions to make your own salsa. You can purchase them from a reliable source, including the grocery store. If you plan to make a lot of salsa, go to the local wholesale market if there is one within driving distance. You will be able to buy a lot more tomatoes, peppers, and onions for your money.

Learn to buy according to what you can actually produce. You want to use your vegetables as soon as possible, but not more than a day or two after you purchase them. Consumers expect freshly made foods to be made from the best ingredients, and that includes vegetables that haven't been hanging around.

THINGS TO CONSIDER

You need a lot of stamina to work in the perishable foods industry! Salsa has become popular, and you will need to plan for a lot of competition, some of it already established. You might want to find some way to stand out from the crowd, although if your salsa is excellent, word of mouth will get you started.

Also, you must learn proper canning techniques in order to prevent the bacteria *Clostridium botulinum* from growing in your salsa. This is critical, because this bacteria produces a deadly toxin.

HOW DO YOU WANT TO SPEND YOUR DAY?

You won't spend all of your time preparing salsa, although there is a lot of chopping and dicing in your future if you plan to make salsa your business. You will also need to bottle, label, market, and deliver your product. And no matter what you do for a business, there are some bookkeeping details to attend to.

WHAT YOU WILL NEED

You will a commercial-sized food processor to chop your vegetables. You'll also need stainless steel bowls in which to mix your salsa. Have at the ready the right containers—you can choose to have different sizes or keep it simple and just make one size all the time.

Be sure to have a good supply of labels; you don't want to have salsa ready to go only to find that you have to wait two days for more labels to be printed!

You will need to have a vehicle to deliver your salsa (probably packed in coolers), although whatever vehicle you own should do it unless you become so big you need a large, refrigerated truck!

MARKETING ANGLE

Marketing salsa can be as time consuming as making it. However, even the biggest grocery stores are looking to add locally-made products to their shelves. Many have created special sections in their stores for organic and natural foods, as well as locally grown and made products such as breads, bakery items, and things such as salsa.

A fun and attractive label will be eye-catching and help your salsa stand out from what is becoming a crowd. Also, adding a small booklet of ideas on how to use your salsa will turn customers into repeat customers.

Consider packaging carefully. Plastic containers are more cost effective than glass. Many homemade salsas are made and sold as fresh: They need to be refrigerated, and they have a modest shelf life. Be clear with your distributors about how you will deal with unsold inventory. It can take a while to get a handle on how much they will sell, but as is the case with most fresh perishables, it is better to have them sell out than provide them with too much inventory that you have to take back and toss.

NICE TOUCH

A nice touch for your salsa business is to make it out of your own "organically grown" produce. Tomatoes, onions, and peppers are quite easy to grow.

EXPANSION POSSIBILITIES

Your expansion possibilities include adding different kinds of salsa to your offerings. Where there is salsa, there needs to be chips; you could also make your own tortilla chips.

WORDS TO KNOW

Salsa: In Spanish, salsa simply means sauce. Americans think of it specifically as the chopped vegetable dip served with Mexican foods.

Cilantro: The leaves of the coriander herb used to flavor many salsas.

RESOURCES

containerandpackaging.com
culinarycafe.com
salsa-recipes.com

38 NUT SALES

Who doesn't love nuts? They provide a delicious and nutritious snack. They add pizzazz to just about every food, from brownies to cereal to salads. And if you coat them with candy, like Jordan almonds, or bury them in chocolate, they are even more irresistible.

You can make a small business out of selling packaged nuts in office buildings. Check with the building owner or property manager to see if it would be OK for you to approach the businesses in the building to sell nuts as snacks to their workers. Once you get the green light to be in the building, check with the appropriate person at each office in the building. Ask if it would be OK for you to come by on a specific day each week at a specific time to sell your snacks to their employees. If you can assure them that you will be efficient about it and not be disruptive, you will most likely get permission from them as well.

Find a nut supplier and stock up on just a few of many different kinds of nuts and nut/candy combinations. The supplier can tell you what tends to be their most popular items; trail mix, for example, is one type of nut snack that sells well.

Experiment with others. Don't be afraid to ask your customers what they would like you to carry and what they like the best. It will benefit you both for you to carry the products they want to buy.

THINGS TO CONSIDER

Be sure to accumulate a few large customers, because if you lose one, which you will, it will put a huge dent in your sales. You need to have enough customers, in a variety of sizes and locations, so that losing one won't have a devastating impact.

HOW DO YOU WANT TO SPEND YOUR DAY?

Most likely, you will be tootling around to several different places during the course of your day. You should enjoy the kind of day where you are never in one place for very long.

That said, you will want to coordinate your stops so that you are in one area one day of the week and another area the next—or even one place just in the morning, another in the afternoon. Once you have some territories established, you will figure out the best way to be efficient.

WHAT YOU WILL NEED

The first thing you will need is a vehicle. You will want something that easily accommodates those square plastic storage tubs. This can help you easily organize your different snacks. It would also be helpful to be able to fit a hand truck in your vehicle to use to wheel several tubs in the building at once.

One of the most cost-effective ways to do this business is to buy your nuts and snacks in bulk and divide them into smaller bags yourself. To do this, you will need a supply of plastic bags and a heat sealer.

After they are sealed, they will need to be labeled so people know what they are buying. You could just use a permanent market to write on the bag what is in it, but you can easily create stick-on labels on a computer—and this would look more neat and professional.

Don't forget; even though they are snacks, this is still food. The more professional looking it is, the more trustworthy people will find your snacks.

MARKETING ANGLE

Although nuts are not low-fat, they are healthy. Promote this aspect of them. And even nuts that are covered with candy can be a healthier snack than the candy alone!

Also, you may want to carry a supply of general nuts, such as chopped walnuts, and remind people that they may want to do some baking over the weekend.

NICE TOUCH

A nice touch in any food business is to give customers the chance to try new things. If your supplier offers something you have never carried—wasabi peas or berry-flavored yogurt-covered raisins—buy some and divide them into small sample bags that you sell for a small amount of money.

Let people try something new without taking too much of a risk. They will not feel badly about spending a dollar on something they decide they don't like. But nuts can be expensive, so people will be less likely to try something if it is $6.95.

EXPANSION POSSIBILITIES

Expanding in this business is often a matter of carrying new items such as branching out from nuts to include popcorn, chips, and other snack foods. Beware that you don't dilute your marketing angle, though. If you are relying on the healthy aspect of your nut business, be sure to add only items that are also healthy.

Another way to expand is to create static displays of your nut snacks to be sold in the offices you also visit—you can restock the display and sell your usual other items. And you can always offer the service of creating gift baskets of your nut and snack items: Take orders one week while you are in the building and deliver them the next.

WORDS TO KNOW

Peanuts: technically not a nut, peanuts are a legume like beans and peas.

Omega-3: A type of fatty acid prevalent in nuts that is considered "good cholesterol" and has been thought to help aid in lowering the risk of coronary heart disease.

Trail mix: A combination of nuts, seeds, dried fruits, candied fruits, and small candies like M&Ms that are mixed together and considered good for a quick pick-me-up while hiking.

RESOURCES

nutsonline.com: a retailer and wholesaler of nuts

nutsite.com

39 COMMUNITY RESTAURANT GUIDE

Most communities have a wealth of restaurants that range from dingy diners to white tablecloth dining establishments. And dining out continues to be a common outlet for disposable income. You could provide residents and visitors alike with a guide to the restaurants available in an area.

If your area doesn't have enough restaurants to make a guide worthwhile, consider roaming a little farther. People will travel to dine at interesting restaurants that have quality food prepared in creative ways. And they will travel to celebrate birthdays and anniversaries with a special dinner at places they've never been.

Your guide will help them decide if the trip is going to be worth it. You should plan to include:

- the restaurant's name, full address, phone number, and website address
- what kind of cuisine the restaurant serves, especially if it is not clear by the restaurant's name
- which days the restaurant is open, what hours they keep on each day, and whether they serve breakfast, lunch, dinner, or all three.
- what kind of dress is appropriate for the restaurant
- whether they have a full bar or are BYO
- whether reservations are accepted and recommended
- any signature dishes the restaurant serves
- a sampling of the menu if there is room

Your restaurant guide could include a few reviews and some photos. You could also include other little tidbits, such as a tipping guide. And of course advertisements—which is why you are doing this!

To be included, you can require the restaurants pay for an ad. But don't think that restaurants are the only advertisements you can have in your guide. Anything that would interest consumers is fair game—retail stores near the restaurants in the guide, hair salons, auto repair shops, cooking schools, you name it.

This may be difficult to do for less than $5,000, mostly because of printing costs. But if you have a track record in advertising sales or in printed materials, you can probably do it. Plan to start small. Have a designer work up a few sample pages for a few hundred dollars with the promise they will get the job if your restaurant guide flies. Sell ads and require at least half up front in payment to hold the spot. Offer to create the ad for them, or if they have their own ready-made ad, use it. Then deliver on your promise with a good-looking, interesting piece that consumers will pick up.

One way to get some buzz going about your new guide is to have something unique in it, some sort of added value—a column by a local chef, a recipe from a restaurant, ways to save gas money (to spend on dining out!). Include anything that makes people want to pick up your guide and read it.

THINGS TO CONSIDER

You will need to decide how often your guide will come out. Seasonally (four times a year) is not too frequent, and often enough to include things such as listings of special events in the area and for restaurants to announce new hours, new specials, and seasonal cuisine. Plan to have an index in the guide, both alphabetical by name of the restaurant and by cuisine type.

HOW DO YOU WANT TO SPEND YOUR DAY?

There is no question that to get this kind of business going you will need to be cook, waiter, and chief bottle washer. In order to make money, you need to keep expenses down. Each job for this business tends to be fairly independent of the other, so once you have the ads sold, you can move on to the design. As you go along, think about what you like to do best and plan to eventually hire people to do the rest.

WHAT YOU WILL NEED

You will need a computer to keep track of all the details of this business. Become proficient in one of the spreadsheet software programs and use it to track your scheduling for the guide's release and create a spreadsheet for your ads.

Find a few friends who are good writers and get them to write a few restaurant reviews. Keep in mind that the restaurants are also being asked to pay for ads in the guide, so you don't want to include overly negative reviews. Negative things can be said in a way that leaves readers to decide for themselves: for instance, "the night we were there, the wait staff were stressed from an unexpected huge party and as a result, the service wasn't as prompt as we might have liked."

Once you have ads, reviews, and other copy to include in the guide, you will need to find a place to print it. Get bids from at least three printers. Don't forget, the cheapest bid is not always the best one. You need someone reliable who is going to meet your deadline. And you need to meet theirs. It makes their lives difficult if you are late getting them your material.

Lastly, you will need to deliver your guide to the places where you arranged to distribute it. Give it away for free, and let the ads pay for it.

MARKETING ANGLE

The main marketing angle for a restaurant guide is that typically consumers have many choices when it comes to deciding where to spend their dining-out dollars. You need to convince restaurants that your guide is a key resource for consumers to figure out what restaurant to patronize.

NICE TOUCH

If you can find the funds, purchase a display rack for your guide so it is readily seen by customers and remains neat and looks inviting. A printed piece that is strewn around looks outdated and not worth picking up.

EXPANSION POSSIBILITIES

By all means, consider expanding to an online presence. You could cover a lot of ground this way and most likely it will be less expensive than the print version.

WORDS TO KNOW

Blow-in card: small postcard-size ads that are placed into magazines. While they can be annoying, they are a successful means to get attention and are a type of advertising to consider for a client who wants special attention. You can also do them as "bind-in" cards, where they are bound into the spine of the magazine, but these are more expensive.

Display ad: A display ad is any ad in your printed piece that is not a "classified" listing.

RESOURCES

restaurantrow.com: "The world's largest dining guide."

restaurantguide.com

40) EDIBLE GIFTS

Practical is a important concept these days. How can you express your appreciation or congratulations with something practical? Send an edible gift! There's nothing more practical than food. And edible gifts allow you to use your creativity to the max.

Of course, giving a box of chocolates is perhaps the granddaddy of all edible gift giving. But fruit arrangements made to look like a bouquet of flowers—melons shaped like daisies and strawberries atop long skewers—are an attractive option. And there are other possibilities for edible arrangements: homemade chocolates (always a welcome sight), or fudge can be hardened around a stick, which allows you to use them decoratively. Cookies are also a food item with great flexibility. Again, you can embed Popsicle or lollipop sticks into the dough before it cooks, which allows you to make unique creations.

Another edible gift is the old-fashioned gingerbread house. You don't have to relegate this to Christmas. Making a gingerbread house portrait of a family home can make a great housewarming present. Or mimic something in a favorite children's book and eat the house at a kid's birthday party.

Edible gifts are great fun, and the possibilities are as endless as your own imagination.

THINGS TO CONSIDER

This business involves perishables and edible arrangements often require refrigeration. You need to have stamina to withstand the stress of dealing with perishable items. If you create a menu of specific items, you will quickly learn exactly how much to purchase of each item you use in any one edible creation. And most things are so easy to get these days that you can order a lot of the more perishable items last minute and per order. You may want to keep some extra on hand to cover those unexpected orders. Also, find a storefront that might carry a couple of your creations on consignment. If you end up ordering more than you need for a specific order because the supplier has a minimum, you can make up a couple of extras and display them on consignment.

HOW DO YOU WANT TO SPEND YOUR DAY?

You will spend your days putting food items together into your edible gifts. The hardest part about a business such as this is the rush at holidays such as Mother's Day and Christmas. You can be overwhelmingly busy a few select times a year. Your challenge will be to stay busy all times of the year.

WHAT YOU WILL NEED

Depending on what you decide to offer for edibles, you may need a refrigerator to store perishables. If your business starts to grow, you can purchase a used florist cooler for your finished products.

MARKETING ANGLE

Definitely emphasize the practicality of your edible gifts. People have to eat, and most people love to eat—what better gift to give than one that is edible? There is little waste, and, depending on what you put together, the gift can be nourishing and shared with others.

Don't leave it up to people to think of you when they need to give a gift. Remind them that what you offer would be a perfect graduation gift or a new baby gift. People these days want to have some of the creative thought done for them.

NICE TOUCH

In your delivered edibles, include a coupon for the recipient worth 10 percent off one order. If they enjoyed their gift, the discount coupon can be one more incentive for them to think of you when they need to acknowledge someone.

EXPANSION POSSIBILITIES

One way to expand is to buy into the franchise business, Edible Arrangements has become popular but is still not on every street corner. You will probably have to give up your own edible gifts business, but it may have provided you with the funding to buy into the franchise.

If franchising seems too corporate, you can expand beyond the arrangements idea and sell edible gifts and tins, and perhaps incorporate the edible gift baskets idea covered earlier.

WORDS TO KNOW

Dipped: One way to dress up an edible arrangement is to include chocolate-dipped berries.

Tower: A popular type of arrangement where multiple containers, each slightly smaller than the last, contain different items and are stacked and tied at the top.

RESOURCES

ediblearrangements.com: the king of the edible arrangement concept

ftd.com: a floral delivery system

FOOD DELIVERY

41

People can have difficulty getting out to get food for any number of reasons: temporary or permanent handicap, people in rural or even suburban areas who don't drive, elderly people. Perhaps some people just don't have the time to shop.

Food delivery can be a business similar to a personal shopper. Since most people have certain brands they like for certain foods, most of the shopping list will be easy to purchase—Starbuck's decaf French Roast, Dinty Moore beef stew, Ben & Jerry's Chunky Monkey ice cream, and so on.

Maybe you live in an area where there is a seasonal population—perhaps you could shop for them and stock the pantry of their summer homes right before their arrival. This may be especially appealing to families coming for a week's stay at the camp; there is hardly enough time to relax, let alone fit in something as mundane as shopping for groceries. They could arrive to a stocked refrigerator and head right out to the lake instead of first making a trip to the store.

Property management companies might be a good source for potential clients for this type of business. They are hired to open the home up before their customers come for a stay. They may not be willing to hand out their customers' names, but you could give them brochures or business cards and ask to be recommended to their clients.

Regular groceries aren't the only food items you can provide. Perhaps your client is having a party and doesn't have the time to shop for all the items they need. You can make a trip to the liquor store, the bakery, the specialty meat store, and the seafood market.

The possibilities are endless. But whatever you decide, you need to be incredibly organized. It will help to know the area well including where the best shops are for the types of items your clients want.

THINGS TO CONSIDER

If you decide to take on a lot of clients, try to find them in the same area to help conserve gas and time; you'll work more efficiently than you could with them scattered here and there.

Plan to pack a couple of large coolers in your vehicle for cold and frozen items. You may have to make several deliveries, and you don't want the last person's ice cream to melt.

HOW DO YOU WANT TO SPEND YOUR DAY?

You need to enjoy spending your day running errands. If you hate grocery shopping for yourself, you certainly aren't going to like to do it for others. You also will need to enjoy organizing and having a structured day. You should plan to be prompt, and your clients will need to be there when you arrive and put perishables away, unless they are willing to give you a key to their home and you are willing to accept that responsibility.

WHAT YOU WILL NEED

Be sure you have a gas-efficient vehicle that is convenient for grocery shopping—hatchbacks are perfect.

You need to have a system in place to divide groceries so you can easily distinguish which bags belong to whom. Perhaps you can color code your clients and purchase colored stickers to put on each bag—anything to make it more efficient and to make sure you are leaving the right groceries with the right customer.

MARKETING ANGLE

In many instances, this service is an extravagance—so you need to make it appear to be a very worthwhile extravagance! Market yourself as making clients' lives easier. Have your customers send their shopping list to you via e-mail. You just print it out when you are ready to go—and you won't have to worry about being able to read their writing!

NICE TOUCH

If you have regular grocery customers, provide them with their own canvas bags for environmentally friendly shopping. You can buy two sets and always have one set in your car; when you deliver those groceries, you take the other empty set with you.

EXPANSION POSSIBILITIES

Probably the best way to expand this business is to become more and more efficient in order to fit in as many customers as possible. You can start small with just groceries and then expand into other kinds of shopping for your customers—or even other services, such as bringing their lawnmower to be fixed or the dog to the groomer.

WORDS TO KNOW

PayPal: A system for payment for online sales. This may be just the thing to check into to get your delivery business website-friendly.

Change order: Instructions to revise a plan or standing order. This is easy to do if your business is organized online, but customers will have to be given a deadline after which it is too late to change their order.

RESOURCES

campusdeliveryassociates.com

delivery.com

wegoshop.com

42 FISH TACOS

Fish tacos have been a hit on the west coast for a while but they have yet to become a generally popular item in the rest of the country. Why not create a new sensation in your town? This is the kind of food that would make a great seasonal stand in town or in their classic setting: being sold from a stand at the beach.

Many recipes for fish tacos can be found on the internet. You can use one of these, customize one, or create your own fresh take by using ingredients that are local to your region—lobster tacos, Maryland crab tacos, the potential is endless!

The traditional fish used in Mexico and the Baja for fish tacos is tilapia. This warm water fish is relatively new to the American fish consumer. The tilapia's white flesh is firm, making it a good texture to use in tacos.

Fish tacos are typically served with salsa, avocado, pico de gallo, yogurt, and a cabbage slaw all wrapped up in a tortilla.

THINGS TO CONSIDER

Fish is not an easy food to manage when it comes to keeping it fresh and estimating how much to have on hand. You need to be comfortable working with perishables. It will take a while for you to learn how much to order and stock. However, from the business owner's perspective, it is better to run out and shut your stand down early than to be over optimistic and throw ingredients away. If you operate a beachside fish taco stand, post your hours as, say, "11:30 a.m. until the fish runs out."

Devoted customers will begin to learn that they need to get to your stand early to get their taco!

HOW DO YOU WANT TO SPEND YOUR DAY?

Don't forget that making and serving fish tacos is only part of your work in this business. You will be on the phone and computer ordering supplies, running around picking up those supplies that can't be delivered, and perhaps driving to the commercial fish market once a week to get the best price on fish.

WHAT YOU WILL NEED

The most important thing to consider is you will need a way to fry your fish. If you want to sell your tacos seaside, you will need to rent a small storefront stand. This may rule out the idea of wheeling a cart down to the beach itself. But why relegate fish tacos only to the beach? It's time they were brought to those places that haven't already embraced them! Customers who associate being on vacation along the shore with eating fish tacos will delight in finding they can have their fish taco at home as well. And they will delight in introducing their friends to this great idea.

MARKETING ANGLE

If you are in an area where fish tacos are not common, your marketing angle will be to challenge people to try something new. You may need to offer a free sample to lure them in. Or consider teaming up with a local bar and having a fish taco sampler night, thereby introducing a whole new audience to this culinary delight.

NICE TOUCH

If fish tacos are new in your area, have a fish taco celebration and get people hooked!

EXPANSION POSSIBILITIES

You could offer to make fish tacos for Mexican-themed parties. Or you could hire yourself out to make fish tacos in a Mexican restaurant in your town. If you don't mind giving away your trade secrets, you could offer classes in cooking fish tacos. The fun of that is coming up with new ideas all the time for making the tacos just a little bit different.

WORDS TO KNOW

Aquaculture: The raising of fish in "farms."

Cichlid: Cichlidae is the family to which the Tilapia genus (which consists of hundreds of members) belongs.

RESOURCES

allrecipes.com

bajafishtacos.net

BOBA STAND

Another food delight that has made it in California, but hasn't moved east in any significant way, is boba. This delicious Asian drink is called bubble tea, although boba and bubble tea are used interchangeably. Bubble tea originated in Taiwan; bubble tea shops have become common all over Asia and are spreading to the rest of the world. You might consider getting in on it as it becomes popular in the U.S.

Bubble tea's name comes from the bubbling process commonly used to make some types of bubble tea. Boba refers to the balls of tapioca found at the bottom of the drink. The boba is sucked up through straws of varying sizes, depending on the size of the balls.

The tea is made in many different ways, but is typically sweet. The tapioca pearls are also sweet; their sweetness derived from ingredients such as caramel, sweet potato, and brown sugar.

As boba becomes more popular, supplies are getting easier to find. The whole operation is quite simple—the most complicated thing you need is a refrigerator and freezer to either make or store ice.

THINGS TO CONSIDER

One thing to consider is that you will be working all the time with the same product. This can get boring for some people but others may see a challenge in finding unique ways to present the same concoction. Boba tea, for instance, has spun off into smoothies and fruit drinks. Perhaps there is something else unique that can be done with tapioca pearls—bury them in custards? Cheesecake? Who's to say coffee drinks can't benefit from a tapioca pearl or two? The trick is not to feel like you can only do something in the way it has always been done.

HOW DO YOU WANT TO SPEND YOUR DAY?

You will spend your day mixing and pouring drinks. You'll need to find time to do your ordering—an important task for any food business.

WHAT YOU WILL NEED

You will need the ingredients to make your boba tea, including tea and milk and perhaps fruit if you decide to offer "smoothie" type boba drinks. The tapioca pearls are a must. You will also need clear drink cups (to show off the black pearls resting at the bottom of the cup!) and the bubbled tops with the large opening to accommodate a large straw to suck up the large pearls. You will also need to provide napkins.

You can do this simple business in either a wheeled cart or other simple stand or in a very modest retail location.

There are a couple of boba franchises open, so you can consider the franchise route if you have the financing and you want a lot of the up-front business done for you already.

Since you will be operating from some kind of retail location—whether it is a small kiosk in the mall or a wheeled cart in the town square—you will need some way to take cash and make change. If you are out in the square, it would be good to have a way to still do business even in inclement weather, although you may find that even though you have shelter for your boba stand, you don't attract enough people to make it worth your while.

MARKETING ANGLE

One important thing you will need to consider is what time of day people are inclined to buy your boba drinks. You don't want to be out there with your stand set up at 6 a.m. to find that most tea drinkers are late afternoon purchasers. And it may be different from one area to another.

If you are in a market too small to sustain your business, and have a moveable stand, you might choose different places to be on different days. People in one area will come to know that you are there on Mondays, another on Tuesdays.

NICE TOUCH

A nice touch with your boba drinks is to offer fresh mint, especially if you begin to sell smoothie or fruit drinks. You could easily grow your own mint and clip some daily—don't forget to wash it well!

EXPANSION POSSIBILITIES

There are several possible expansion ideas for a boba drink stand. You could add stands and hire people to run them for you, especially if you have been rotating to different markets each day and think you could now have enough customers in one market to stay there all the time. Extra stands cost more to run, because you have to stock them all and pay help, but it can significantly help your profit margin by allowing you to order supplies in larger quantities and get better discounts on your purchases.

WORDS TO KNOW

Dome lids: Plastic cup lids that are dome-shaped and usually have an oversized hole to allow the large straw typically served with boba.

Pearls: The tapioca balls that are an integral part of boba.

RESOURCES

boba.com

bubbleteasupply.com

44 KIDS' BIRTHDAY TREATS

What fun it could be to spend your time making entertaining treats for kids' birthdays! The possibilities are endless: Specialty birthday cakes with trains, horses, or other themes are great fun to create. Cakes made out of cupcakes, green-dyed coconut as grass for a horse pasture, train tracks made out of string licorice... and cakes are just the beginning. Cookies lend themselves to a great many different decorations, from frosting to candies and beyond.

Parents will love you if you create with treats that at least border on healthy. Consider decorating granola bars instead of sugar cookies. Popcorn is always a popular treat and is typically a little healthier than other snacks.

The main thing is making them look fun and appealing. Take any kid past the bakery counter at the grocery store, and it would be rare if they didn't plead for one of those sugar cookies decorated to look like the Cookie Monster, Santa Claus, or a sunflower. They look so yummy. You need to figure out what will make your treats fun and yummy, too.

One way to think of what kinds of themes to focus on is to go shopping. Spend some time in a toy store and see what kids are into these days. Parents who spend significant amounts of money on their child's birthday party will want to make sure that the latest hot trend is well represented.

Another place to shop is the children's section of the bookstore. Not only can you find out the latest hot super star (think Harry Potter—what kid's birthday party didn't revolve around a wizard theme over the past eight or so years?), but you can also be reminded of the old standbys that kids always enjoy: Beatrix Potter, The Little Engine That Could, Charlie and the Chocolate Factory, Bambi, and hundreds of other classic are always popular.

THINGS TO CONSIDER

You should start your enterprise using your own children, grandchildren, nieces, nephews, or friends' kids as guinea pigs. Experiment to determine what they like and don't like, especially if you plan to focus on more healthy treats.

You can also solicit ideas from the kids: have a little focus group. Gather a few kids together and present them with samples of your treats. Make two of each: one that they can just look at and make comments on, another that you cut up into pieces, let them eat, and give you their reaction to the taste. Plan to have a helper—someone who can write down the children's comments and reactions, while you interact with them and get them to talk about the different aspects of the treats.

HOW DO YOU WANT TO SPEND YOUR DAY?

This is a business where your days can be pretty divided among several different tasks. First, you will need to spend time marketing your birthday treats. Once you have customers, you will need to spend time researching recipes and making the treats themselves.

If you enjoy the fun of being around the kids, you will want to organize your business so that you deliver the treats. Consider offering a package of entertainment and treats or actually conducting kids parties, treats included.

WHAT YOU WILL NEED

First and foremost, you will need marketing materials. Put posters up at the grocery store, toy stores, and any place parents frequent. A website is always a good idea. You will need to make some samples to photograph for your flyers and website. And you will need to spend a lot of time developing creative ideas that tempt parents to come to you rather than just picking something up at the bakery.

You will need to have order forms printed. Once you have an order, you will need to purchase your supplies. Some supplies you can purchase ahead of time and have on hand. But much of what you need will be perishable, so don't purchase too much in advance, unless you have several orders in hand.

MARKETING ANGLE

If you choose to focus on healthy treats for kids, be sure to market that! Parents will love it. And you need to explain to them why the kids will love them, too—that they taste sweet or look fun or have something hidden inside. Whatever you decide, your main marketing challenge is going to be making sure your product appeals to both the children who are going to eat them and the adults who are going to buy them.

Another aspect of marketing this kind of business is that there are fewer repeat customers than with other businesses. Not that you won't get repeat business, but a kid has a birthday only once a year. Your repeat business may come in the form of sibling birthday parties, but sometimes parents duplicate for one child what they did for the other, and sometimes they go out of their way to make each child's birthday quite different in order for each to feel they got something special.

NICE TOUCH

Always add a little something extra, especially when you are dealing with kids and parents. Balloons are a nice touch. If you based your treats on a book-inspired theme, purchase a copy of the book to give as a gift to the birthday child. Or, presuming they are a fan of that theme and they probably already have the book, purchase a copy and donate it to the local library or shelter in the birthday child's name.

EXPANSION POSSIBILITIES

The expansion possibilities are a little limited with this kind of business because there are only so many birthdays you can handle at a time. One way to expand, however, is to make extras of your birthday treats and find a retail outlet that will sell them for you. You could also expand your birthday offerings beyond just treats and create a whole birthday package that parents can buy "off the shelf."

WORDS TO KNOW

Allergen: Something that causes an allergic reaction. Peanuts are now a common and sometimes life-threatening allergen for kids and should be avoided in any food items for children.

Piñatas: Piñatas are made of paper mache and can be any shape. They are filled with treats, usually candy. Kids take turns hitting the hanging piñata while they are blindfolded until it bursts open and spills the treats to the ground.

RESOURCES

artistshelpingchildren.org
kinderinfo.com

45 TORTILLA CHIPS

The popularity of tortilla chips has exploded and doesn't appear to be going away anytime soon. You can jump on this bandwagon and make your own as a business. Tortilla chips are fun and easy. And they don't have to be plain and boring—you can get as creative you want with things such as seasonings or packaging.

THINGS TO CONSIDER

Making homemade tortillas on your home stove or oven is fine, but will take longer than it would with a commercial-size appliance. First, you will need to figure out how many sales you have and what you need to fill your orders. Perhaps you are only supplying your local natural foods convenience store to start. This is manageable. But if you want to spread your wings beyond that, you need to get serious with a commercial oven and some open space to cut, package, and store your chips. Packaging can be tricky as you need to be able to vacuum pack chips. Search around for a place that can do this for you or start off small with a small packaging machine. You will also need to consider delivery of your chips to the markets with whom you have set up accounts.

You will want to find a tortilla supplier and be able to purchase tortillas in quantity to get them at a great price.

HOW DO YOU WANT TO SPEND YOUR DAY?

You will spend a lot of time making tortilla chips. If the actual cooking is the part of this business you like best, great. Otherwise, you should find some help with this aspect while you do what you like—marketing, merchandising, whatever.

WHAT YOU WILL NEED

The main thing you will need is the tortillas. A lot of them. Making the chips is pretty simple: You cut them up, and one tortilla makes at least eight chips. You deep fry the tortilla wedges in oil heated to between 375 and 400 degrees Fahrenheit. Use a slotted spoon to scoop them out once they are crispy but not brown. Blot them to get the excess oil off; paper towels work, but you may want to find a more commercially viable product for the fat absorption since you will be making large quantities.

Lower fat tortilla chips can be made by spraying the tortilla wedges with a cooking spray and baking them in the oven.

The real fun part comes in seasoning the chips. Salt, of course, is typical but you can use celery salt, cinnamon, a commercially available special seasoning mix like Mrs. Dash, or whatever strikes your fancy!

Once you have your tortillas made, you will need to have a way to package them. You will want to decide whether you are going to create individual serving sizes (a thing not commonly done with tortilla chips) or put them in large bags.

MARKETING ANGLE

Try teaming up with a salsa maker to either sell your products together or to do reciprocal coupons or marketing materials to include with each others' products. Approach your local sub shop to see if they would carry your tortilla chips, packaged in lunch-size portions, on the counter to tempt their sub customers to buy your locally made chips as opposed to the regular potato chip offerings.

NICE TOUCH

Use environmentally sound packaging for your tortilla chips. It's not only good for the environment, it's good for marketing your business.

Put interesting copy on your packaging, something that is worth reading. People are always looking for something to read with their lunch. Cereal boxes have made an art form out of it. Find something worthwhile to put on the bag—ten ways to make your home more energy efficient, six ideas for using the internet, whatever suits your fancy!

EXPANSION POSSIBILITIES

If you are making tortilla chips, other kinds of chips are always a good next step. Chips made out of sweet potatoes or pita bread are gaining in popularity. Or, if you haven't found a salsa maker to team up with, consider making your own. Guacamole is another common tortilla chip condiment you could make. Design party platters with chips, salsa, and guacamole for an easy "potluck" purchase for a busy partygoer.

You can also expand your production capabilities. If you can save up some money by starting slowly, you might be able to get the working capital you need to move into a commercially viable space with more production capabilities. And you will need some help!

WORDS TO KNOW

Merchandising: How a product is displayed in the store. For example, chips are best displayed near the checkout counter as an impulse purchase.

Sealers: A wide variety of sealers are available to seal your chip bags before they end up on the store shelf.

RESOURCES

abouteating.com

recipezaar.com

Every kitchen needs a cutting board, or even two or three. Cutting boards can be easy to make, and you can decorate them in almost any possible fashion.

You can use different kinds of wood to make your cutting boards. If you don't feel comfortable making cutting boards from scratch, you can have the basic piece cut for you so you can concentrate on the final details of sanding, finishing the edges, oiling, and any kind of decorating you want to do.

THINGS TO CONSIDER

When making cutting boards, be sure to consider how they are used. You don't want to carve intricate details that are going to trap food and make them difficult to clean. Keep your cutting area clear and smooth.

Don't use stains or dyes to color your cutting boards; always keep in mind that people will be using them to work with food.

HOW DO YOU WANT TO SPEND YOUR DAY?

This is a business where you spend a lot of time alone working in your wood shop. You need to be OK with that! Your main interactions with people will be in marketing your products to potential sales outlets.

You also will spend a lot of time with loud power tools. Always concentrate on safety, including

- buying the latest model tool that has all the latest safety features

- wearing safety glasses and hearing protection devices

- keeping your shop free of excess sawdust to prevent fire

- keeping your shop neat and clear of clutter in order to avoid tripping

- learning how to operate your power tools safely and accurately

WHAT YOU WILL NEED

If you plan to create cutting boards from the beginning of the process, you will need a table saw, planer, and router to create the basic board. You can get creative and have some fun by using templates to shape your cutting boards into fun designs such as animal figures, fruit shapes, or other kitchen-appropriate shapes such as the cross section of a loaf of bread or a teapot.

MARKETING ANGLE

It's hard to come up with something unique about cutting boards, but they can be found in almost every household, so the market is huge! With the recent emphasis on food safety, many people will want two or three cutting boards in their kitchen: one for meat, one for fruits and vegetables, and one for breads. Maybe even a fourth for using as an hors d'oeuvres platter.

Use this marketing angle to promote purchasing several cutting boards. In fact, you can package together set of four cutting boards, each for a different purpose. Promote these as great housewarming gifts.

You should be sure to have a website. Cutting boards are easy enough to ship, so being able to sell from your website will be important.

NICE TOUCH

For those people who do use different cutting boards for different foods, it would be nice to have cutting boards that made it clear which is for what, especially when it comes to meat. First, it makes it easy to grab the one you need. Also, if you have guests or a housesitter, they will automatically know which particular cutting board is used for what.

Also, you could create a cutting board especially for meat that has plastic cutting board insert that can be taken out and run through the dishwasher.

EXPANSION POSSIBILITIES

Once you sell cutting boards, you can start to expand into other wood products such as coasters, kitchen wall hangings with those funny little sayings on them, or whatever strikes your fancy! Try adding a small cheese knife to your cheese cutting board. Create more elaborate cutting boards. You could even turn to custom cutting boards for people with special needs such as a countertop with a big hole in it where a countertop stove was removed or to cover a large burn mark, stain, or crack.

WORDS TO KNOW

Planer: A woodworking hand tool used to smooth, flatten, or thin a piece of wood.

Router: A woodworking tool used to create grooves and divots in a piece of wood by hollowing them out with sharp bits of varying sizes.

RESOURCES

toolcrib.com: free cutting board plans

woodworkersworkshop.com: cutting board plans

woodworkingtools.com

47 VINTAGE KITCHENWARE

Vintage anything will be forever popular as long as the right person is matched up with the item. People purchase vintage items because they derive nostalgic pleasure from seeing something they associate with their mother's or grandmother's kitchen. Or they remember using an item as a child and enjoy having it in their own kitchen. Some people have decorated their kitchens specifically in vintage style and purchase items with their theme. Some collect vintage items with the hope that they will some day be worth more than they paid for them. All of these reasons will make them seek out your vintage kitchenware collection.

This is a business you can do via the internet and your own website or even just over eBay. You could sell things via a yard sale or out of your garage, but people often expect to pay less for items at yard sales, so if you have nice things and want to get a good price for them, a yard sale isn't the way to go.

Your kitchenware could include dishware, small appliances such as mixers and toasters that flap open on each side, real silverware, cast iron skillets—the list is endless.

THINGS TO CONSIDER

Most of your items will be small—nesting bowls, wooden-handled utensils, butter molds, and so on. But you may find some larger items interest you—soapstone sinks and Hoosier-style baking cupboards, for example, will take a little more shipping creativity than a wooden-handled utensil.

Check with the shipping services most convenient to you about how much it would cost to ship an item and whether they would actually do it before you decide to fill your garage with 400-pound soapstone sinks!

HOW DO YOU WANT TO SPEND YOUR DAY?

A lot of your time will be spent shopping around "antique" and flea market type shops looking for vintage kitchenware items. For someone who enjoys shopping, this will be great fun and not a hardship at all. If you choose to open a retail shop, you will spend a good amount of time in the shop, which makes online selling appealing since it can be done any time of the day or night, including while you are off looking for inventory.

WHAT YOU WILL NEED

You will need a good supply of vintage items to sell. Check estate sales in the paper, moving sales, and be sure to rummage through that junk shop at the traffic circle that you go by every week on your way to your daughter's ball game.

You can start your selling as soon as you have even just one item (don't forget to rummage through your own house, too, and those of your friends and family who are looking to clean their attics). However, it is better to have a few items before you start to market yourself as a vintage seller, because you will want to keep your name and business out there at all times.

Get a digital camera and take good photos of the items you have for sale so you can post them on eBay and other sites as well as your own website. In order to best show off your item, you will want some fabric that can provide you with a plain backdrop; buy fabrics in different colors like blue, green, and white or cream in order to be able to set off any color item. Make sure the fabric is cotton or something without a sheen so there is no glare in your photo.

To take the best photos of small kitchenware, you will want a couple of inexpensive reflective lights to get rid of shadows, to show off the real color of the item, and to showcase any interesting details such as small wooden handles or decorative etching on metal pieces.

If you decide to sell retail as well as online, you will want some sort of storefront. One great way to do this is to work in a co-op situation where several vintage sellers get together and rent a room in a antique dealer's building. This is a great way to share things such as utility expenses and to share shopkeeping time, where only one or two of the co-op members need to be in the shop at any given time.

You don't need to buy special display racks to show off your collectibles— just put things on tables or even large pieces of kitchen furniture such as tables and buffet cabinets to display your smaller items.

MARKETING ANGLE

Definitely play to people's nostalgia! Emphasize the fact that older items are often better made and involve more stylish detail than a lot of modern items. Be sure that you are listed in any antiques listings. Take out small ads in antique newspapers. Do website link exchanges. Consider starting a "kitchen collectibles" blog and promote your collection that way.

NICE TOUCH

If you find magazine photos of an item you have for sale or even a magazine article, include it when you sell the item. Or do research and write up a short informational piece about the item and send that along when it is sold. Buyers will appreciate anything they can learn about any vintage item they purchase.

EXPANSION POSSIBILITIES

The expansion possibilities with this business come with expanding your offerings. You will, of course, have to consider how much space you have—you need to sell as fast as you buy! If you get the opportunity to buy a collection, for instance at an estate sale, consider renting a storage unit to contain any overflow that you can't keep either in a co-op retail situation or at your home.

WORDS TO KNOW

Mortar and pestle: kitchen tools made of wood, metal, or stone that are used to hand grind small amounts of spices or grains.

Fiesta dinnerware: A vintage art deco style dishware in bright colors made by the Homer Laughlin China Company. Designed in 1936, it is among the most collected chinaware in the world; it was discontinued in 1973 but reissued in 1986.

RESOURCES

atticshoppe.com
ebay.com

48 HEALTHY FAST FOOD

Fast food is here to stay, but even the huge fast food franchises have recognized that Americans have become concerned with unhealthy eating habits. Restaurants have been expanding their menus to contain healthy salads and wraps along with their usual offerings of super-sized hamburgers and fries.

Why make consumers shuffle through a fat-laden menu to look for the healthy selections? They get the salad, but are tempted to throw in a small order of those irresistible french fries. If all that was offered was healthy selections, there would be no temptation. That is where you come in.

A small kiosk in the middle of a parking lot on a busy road could become a great destination for those who seek a healthy lunch alternative. Healthy lunch selections mean you would have no need for things such as fryolators that take up space and cost a lot to run.

You could make sandwiches and salads ahead of time somewhere else where there is more space and have refrigeration to store them in your kiosk. Or, if you set your kiosk up incredibly efficiently, you could make your healthy sandwiches to order.

Keep your selections small. Even the big chains such as Subway have gotten carried away with selections. Most people find something they really like and only ever buy that one thing, anyway. Keep it simple. Offer, say, five sandwiches—three meat selections and two vegetarian—and a couple of different kinds of salads. Keep them healthy by using things such as hummus spread instead of mayonnaise. Offer salads with the dressing on the side, so customers can monitor their own salad dressing intake. Sell water and diet soda, and perhaps pita chips or baked potato chips as a lower fat alternative to regular chips.

THINGS TO CONSIDER

The hardest part of this kind of business will be having a kiosk or other storefront site. If that doesn't seem like a reasonable idea in your community, consider trying to sell your healthy selections at a local convenience store instead of opening your own spot. A lot of convenience stores love to have locally made products. Many of them have lunch counters that are no longer operating or are being kept up at a minimum level just because the space is there. These all offer potential for you to take on that aspect of the business for the store and relieve them of the burden. This can be a win-win situation, since your customers will help drive business into the store, and that person having a healthy lunch at your lunch counter may need a carton of milk and a loaf of bread, too!

HOW DO YOU WANT TO SPEND YOUR DAY?

You will spend your day essentially in the restaurant business. If you focus on only lunch, you can cater to the working crowd and concentrate your work time into the lunch period—from 11 a.m. to around 2:30 p.m.

Of course, there is a lot to do on either side of that! If you do lease a lunch counter or have a kiosk, you need to make sure you are keeping track of everything you need to do to keep the health inspectors happy. And you need to spend plenty of time ordering supplies and ingredients, as well as figuring out what kind of marketing you will do.

WHAT YOU WILL NEED

You will need an ample supply of the ingredients for all of the sandwiches and salads you plan to have on your menu. It will take a few weeks to determine which things are bestsellers and which are not. Keep trying new things until you find the right mix of sandwiches that are regular sellers. The key to keeping this as an under-$5,000 startup is to start small and keep it simple.

MARKETING ANGLE

Healthy eating is your main marketing angle. This is the working person's lunch alternative to whipping through the classic fast food drive-through. Be sure you emphasize that your lunches are quick. Distribute flyers at any local businesses where nearby workers can consider you for their lunch break.

NICE TOUCH

Many people who are looking for healthy and low-fat lunches would like some little sweet thing for dessert. Include one of those mini mint patties you find at convenience store counters or some other individually wrapped candy—just enough of a sweet to feel like a dessert. You could even have desserts available but make cookies or other portions on the small side; many people would like a sweet but don't want to purchase a cookie the size of a bicycle tire.

EXPANSION POSSIBILITIES

The best way to do this business is to start small and offer a modest selection. You can then put expansion plans into place to increase the number of lunch selections you offer as well as desserts and sides.

You could also consider conducting classes in healthy eating or bring your expertise to workplaces and conduct seminars there. Many companies would pay you to give a class that would help their employees stay healthy.

WORDS TO KNOW

Loss leader: An item that is sold below cost, or which doesn't make as much profit as other things, but brings people into your store where they presumably become tempted to buy other things.

Chain: A "chain" is a group of stores with a single owner. In the fast food business, you will be competing with chains and "franchises" (chains of individually owned stores that operate under common terms set out by the franchisor), which can be very difficult.

Healthy: This is a loaded term! You can use it to mean almost anything you want, but typically it refers to something about your food offering that provides a health benefit—low in fat, high in nutrition, etc.

RESOURCES

foodnetwork.com
whfoods.com

49 ROMANTIC DINNER CATERING

What a nice way to make a living, helping others have a lovely evening! A romantic catering service can be simple and incredibly creative. Since you probably won't have the same customers more than once a year or so, you can keep your menu very simple.

Become an expert in a half dozen of each of the dinner's courses: Appetizer, soup, salad, main dish, and dessert. Offer a nice range of vegetarian, low-fat, and hearty meals. In summer, have a cold soup selection. Always have at least one dessert selection that even someone who watches calories would order.

Have your couple select from your menu. They can pick and choose a la carte or you can recommend menus that are complementary dishes such as a goat cheese salad with a rack of lamb and lemon chiffon cheesecake.

In order to avoid liquor licensing issues, tell your customers to purchase their own wine and liquor. If you are serving them in their own home, be sure they leave all the liquor in the kitchen and let you know what they want.

If your home has the space and zoning allows it, you could create a one-table dining room. In order to really be romantic, you would want it to be nicely appointed and perhaps overlooking a garden or even have a screened porch or deck off the room. In summer, you could actually serve out there. Include a fireplace, even if it is the gas-fired kind. A bubbling fountain, plants, lush drapes, or maybe even those fake stars on the ceiling (if you can pull it off tactfully), and, of course, music, all help set a romantic mood. In order to charge a significant price tag, you need to have some unique touches that make having a romantic dinner catered by you a wish list item.

THINGS TO CONSIDER

If you will be serving at the customers' home, you will want to check out the premises ahead of time. Also, plan to bring everything you need except the major appliances, as you don't want to interrupt the couples' romantic dinner to ask where they keep the corkscrew, etc.

HOW DO YOU WANT TO SPEND YOUR DAY?

You will be spending a few hours the day of the scheduled dinner purchasing and preparing the food. If you are serving at your home, be sure the dining room is impeccably clean. Don't set the table until shortly before the couple is ready to arrive.

WHAT YOU WILL NEED

If you do your catering at the couple's home, you will want to have a picnic basket full of the dishes, utensils, linens, stemware, and candles for the table (don't forget to bring matches). Make sure you have remembered the things you need to serve appetizers, salads, and all the extras. Bring all the pots and pans you will need, as well as serving utensils. You will need a good-size cooler (or perhaps two medium-sized ones) to keep everything chilled. Don't forget a corkscrew, bottle opener, can opener, and any unique item that your menu might require.

MARKETING ANGLE

Restaurants are busy, crowded, and noisy and the good ones often have a waiting list. Many people would pay extra to be guaranteed a relaxing, quiet, romantic dinner without the hassle and the crowd.

NICE TOUCH

Fresh flowers on the table is a lovely touch. And using fresh herbs, lettuces, and other vegetables from the garden that can be seen from the dining room in your home is always a hit.

EXPANSION POSSIBILITIES

You could expand to have a couple of seatings per evening, or, if you have a room that is big enough, you could artfully partition it with a dressing screen, shoji screen, or just a heavy drape. Each area could have its own theme. You could charge less for being part of a two-seating evening, or you could simply use the extra area to overlap the two seatings—while one is wrapping up, the other is just starting. You might overlap them so that one couple is starting the evening on the porch with drinks and appetizers while the other is wrapping up with dessert and coffee.

WORDS TO KNOW

Aphrodisiac: A food considered to have libido-enhancing properties, such as oysters or chocolate.

Seating: A specified time when a table is occupied. High-end restaurants often offer a defined seatings in order to control the traffic for the evening and be able to provide a special dining experience (for which they can charge high prices).

RESOURCES

sandjcatering.net

travellinggourmet.com

FOOD SAFETY CONSULTANT

50

Food safety is such a big topic in food-related businesses of any kind that this is a make-your-own business. First, you will need to immerse yourself in food safety from all aspects. Selling food to the public is a very complicated and regulated business. Helping restaurants and other food businesses sort out what they need to know and what they need to be paying attention to can be very helpful.

You can promote services such as doing an audit of a new restaurant before the health inspector comes. The benefit for them is that they can be ready to open sooner. For places already in business, offer regular food safety audits. And do it just like the inspectors do—unannounced. List everything that isn't up to snuff—food handlers not wearing hair nets or gloves, walk-in freezers not as clean as they should be, ice machines with scoops left inside on top of the ice. All these little details can add up to black marks on the health inspectors' report.

Provide not only a report that points out inadequacies but also tells them how to rectify the inadequacy. If it involves some piece of equipment, offer some ideas on where to get that equipment at the best cost.

Be as much of a resource to your businesses as you possibly can.

THINGS TO CONSIDER

This kind of business is food-related, but is a step away from actual food. If you want to be involved with food itself, this is not the business for you. However, it can be one of the most important aspects of any food business. Also, you may have to overcome restaurant and food business owners' negative attitudes, since most are not happy to see the health inspector. You will need to emphasize that you are NOT the health inspector and in fact can make their visit with the health inspector much more pleasant.

HOW DO YOU WANT TO SPEND YOUR DAY?

You will spend most of your time on the road in the behind-the-scenes areas of restaurants and food businesses. Somewhere in there, you need to make time to keep abreast of any news and information that will help you help your clients. This may be where having lunch in one of the many places that now offer free wireless internet services will be a boon.

WHAT YOU WILL NEED

Get on alert listings and newsletters that will keep you apprised immediately of anything like the spinach and tomato recalls that have been public health concerns over the past couple of years. Set up an e-mail alert system so that all of your clients have this information immediately. Also, provide them with your analysis of the situation and what your recommendation would be for their business.

MARKETING ANGLE

The marketing angle you need to take with a food safety consulting business is that you will save your clients time and potentially fines and penalties by helping them make sure their businesses are up to snuff when it comes to food safety concerns. And beyond the money aspect, you will save them the unknown penalties of bad press and the negative public perception of a food business with citations from the health inspector.

NICE TOUCH

This is the kind of business where criticism is a built-in factor. A nice touch would be to indicate where your clients are doing things right. This also helps to encourage them to continue to do those things so they won't become part of your report in the future.

Also, be sure to introduce yourself to employees as you go about your business. Don't come across as an adversary; you are there to help them all do their jobs better. No one benefits from either down time or a slowing of business if the facility fails a health inspection.

EXPANSION POSSIBILITIES

Start with a small operation and learn as much about the food safety business as you possibly can both by education opportunities and hands-on experience. Then branch out into larger operations such as chain restaurants, grocery stores, and food producers.

WORDS TO KNOW

Model Food Code: The Food Code is created by the FDA, is extensive, and includes things such as cooking temperatures for meat, how often restaurants should be inspected, equipment standards, etc.

Perishables: Foods that have a short shelf life and/or need to be kept under special conditions, such as refrigeration.

Salmonella: A bacteria that can cause the food-borne illness salmonellosis.

RESOURCES

fda.gov

restaurant.org

There are many printed materials you could create for restaurants—menus and advertisements being just a couple of them. But those paper s with local business ads around the perimeter are a perennial cash cow. People sit at the table waiting for their food to come, and even if they don't realize it, they are staring at the placemat and subconsciously registering the names of several businesses advertised on the placemat. And even after they get their meal, the ads are usually still visible around the edges of the dinner plate.

This business is, of course, not for upscale restaurants—they are using cloth tablecloths, not paper placemats. But that leaves a huge number of middle-scale and diner-type restaurants for whom paper placemats are perfect.

The way it works is that you provide the restaurant with the placemats at a low cost, maybe even just the cost of the printing, or perhaps the design and printing. Then all of the businesses that advertise on the placemat pay an ad rate. The more business a restaurant averages, the more customers who will see the ads, so the more valuable the ad is to the advertiser, and the more you can charge for the ad.

The businesses you approach should be ones that almost everyone uses: Auto repair, home maintenance, and landscaping services are just a few of the possibilities. Don't waste your time trying to get a high-end spa to advertise on the placemat of the local pub.

THINGS TO CONSIDER

Although this is a relatively good business in almost any market, ad sales are tough no matter what you are selling.

This is not directly related to working with food, although you will spend a lot of time in food establishments.

HOW DO YOU WANT TO SPEND YOUR DAY?

You will spend most of your time soliciting advertising. This means quite a lot of travel, although your market area could be fairly small for each placemat you do. Once you have a core group of advertisers, these will mostly be able to be contacted by phone after they have signed on.

WHAT YOU WILL NEED

You will need a computer and sales tracking software to keep track of whom you have approached and with whom you need to follow up, as well as what businesses have signed on for how many printings.

You will definitely need a phone system, even if it is just a cell phone, for business purposes. You also should plan to have a fax machine so you can respond immediately to anything that can't be done via e-mail.

You will also need a reliable vehicle for sales calls. And the vehicle should be of a sort that could carry several boxes of placemats if you are going to deliver them yourself, at least at the beginning.

MARKETING ANGLE

Your first marketing job will be to convince a restaurant that they should use the placemats you plan to create. Then you need to market to businesses that having their ad on a placemat at that particular restaurant is a great use of their advertising dollars because it will reach the people they need to reach.

NICE TOUCH

A nice touch would be to give your placemat company a snappy name that people will remember, and then make sure you have a website that you advertise prominently on the placemat. At your website, potential customers will find all of the people who advertised on your placemat. That way, they don't have to remember the name of the company and or tear off the ketchup-smeared ad and put it in their purse or pocket. They can just remember one snappy name to look up on the internet.

EXPANSION POSSIBILITIES

The main expansion possibilities with this business is to start with one restaurant in one market, then expand to other restaurants (with a different set of businesses) and to other markets.

WORDS TO KNOW

On press: When your printed piece is actually on the printing press being printed.

Bleed: In printing, when the image area extends off the edge of the paper. This design element tends to be more expensive because it requires printing on a larger piece of paper and trimming it down to size.

RESOURCES

mastercraftprinting.com
placematprinters.com

PRETZEL VENDOR

Those hand-rolled, baked hot pretzels with large chunks of salt and a little mustard are hard to resist. You can turn them into a business! Pretzel vendors are found on city street corners, in parks, or at fairs.

Use your friends and family as guinea pigs to create the absolute best pretzel. Experiment with toppings, sizes, thicknesses, and even types of wrap to use. Shop pretzel vendors yourself to see what people are charging. Research other local vendors of other snack items—roasted nuts, bagels, donuts—and come up with a competitive price for your pretzels.

THINGS TO CONSIDER

Unless you set up a permanent retail site, the vending cart business requires a bit of physical stamina.

HOW DO YOU WANT TO SPEND YOUR DAY?

If you go the vending route, you will spend your day out on the street hawking pretzels to passersby. You will need to enjoy interacting with strangers all day long. And you will need to have the stamina to be there all day in all kinds of weather and to get your vending cart to the site, set it up, break it down, and then get it back to its overnight storage location.

WHAT YOU WILL NEED

You will need a cart if that is the way you plan to sell your pretzels. This will be your biggest expense. To keep within the $5,000 limit, you will need to lease your cart unless you can find a great deal on a used one or make an efficient cart yourself. The cart will need a way to heat the pretzels, usually an oven, which usually has a humidified cabinet to hang the pretzels for both display and heating, and you will need to be located within range of an electrical supply or use a generator.

Then you will need the supplies to make the pretzels. This is fairly modest—flour, yeast, baking soda, butter, and whatever kinds of toppings you plan to offer—or you can buy ready-made frozen pretzels.

MARKETING ANGLE

Without the sweet toppings, pretzels are a low-fat, filling snack. Be sure to promote this aspect of this popular snack item, however you plan to sell them.

NICE TOUCH

If you are going the street vendor route, this is a perfect kind of business to offer a loyalty card—buy ten, get the 11th free. It is a great way to get local workers to come to you for their daily afternoon snack rather than shop around to other vendors. If you offer enough different toppings, they will never get bored.

EXPANSION POSSIBILITIES

First, you can expand modestly by simply adding some drinks to your vending cart offerings.

Once you get your own special style of pretzel down, you could expand to sell them online with delivery. Imagine a "pretzelgram" sent to someone with a greeting and a beautiful baked pretzel in a nice box with a couple of packets of toppings and instructions on how to heat it to perfection in the microwave. Or you could get into smaller snacking pretzels dipped in chocolate, white chocolate, or yogurt and sold in attractive tins.

WORDS TO KNOW

Handrolled: Pretzels that are rolled and twisted by hand.

Peels: Long wooden paddles used to remove pretzels from hot ovens.

Sourdough: A leaven (yeast) that causes fermentation in dough to make bread.

RESOURCES

pretzeltime.com: a franchise opportunity

southernconcessionsupply.com: suppliers of pretzel equipment, including frozen, lo-fat, no preservatives frozen pretzels.

53 KITCHEN INCUBATOR

Starting a kitchen incubator is not a cheap proposition. It will be difficult to start up for less than $5,000, but if you really were into the idea, you could start small and build.

The way they work is that a small startup food-related business rents your fully equipped commercial kitchen facility to get their business up and running until they can acquire the capital to build their own facilities. The facility is, of course, shared by several (you hope!) startup businesses that pay for use of the facility. They schedule time slots, so XYZ Pita Chip company might have use of the facility every Monday and Friday from 5am to noon and Felice's Chocolate Chip Cookie Delights has it on Tuesdays and Thursdays all day.

The challenge is to keep the kitchen incubator facility fully rented at almost all times. The utility charges will be considerable, with commercial ovens running 12-18 hours a day. You need to be very realistic about how much to charge for use of the facility, but the trick there is to keep it within reach of the startup business owner.

Some incubators have add-on services such as helping with planning for the business before it starts and as it gets going. You can get creative in how you pay for your facility by doing things such as taking a small share of the business's profits when the business succeeds enough to leave your facility and go out on its own. So the company only pays this money if they actually make it in their business.

THINGS TO CONSIDER

Startup food businesses are very risky ventures. You will want to have a very careful screening process for your potential tenants.

You will need to have a cleaning service that knows how to clean food service areas. Although the individual tenants should be expected to clean up before they leave each time, health inspectors have high expectations, and those expectations need to be met.

HOW DO YOU WANT TO SPEND YOUR DAY?

You will spend your time being a landlord, basically. If you are very organized and enjoy coordinating and the exciting process of starting up businesses, this can be exactly the kind of thing you may want to spend your time doing. There will not be a dull moment, that's for sure.

WHAT YOU WILL NEED

You will need an appropriate space. The good news is, this space doesn't have to be in prime retail rental area. You will want good parking and a safe neighborhood, because if your incubator is to work, there should be people there at all hours of the day and night.

MARKETING ANGLE

The main marketing angle for this business is the incredible opportunity for food entrepreneurs to have a place to start their businesses without the expense of creating a professional kitchen themselves.

NICE TOUCH

Consider holding some business classes specifically for food entrepreneurs. If you cater to a certain kind of food business, such baked goods or healthy foods, tailor your classes to that specialty. These classes can include things about food safety, insurance, or any of the myriad aspects that food entrepreneurs need to know.

EXPANSION POSSIBILITIES

Besides adding more kitchen space to accommodate more entrepreneurs at a time, you can also consider having a small retail space where customers can sample the wares of your tenants.

WORDS TO KNOW

Convection Oven: Specialize ovens that cook food faster by using a circulating fan.

Time Share: Use of a facility for a given time period for a fee. Time shares are conventionally thought of for condominiums, but it is essentially the same concept with a kitchen incubator.

RESOURCES

americastestkitchen.com: The test kitchen site for *Cook's Illustrated* magazine

mikitchenessukitchen.com

testkitchens.com

AMERICAN CULTURAL FOODS

54

O K, this is a bit "out there", but what the heck, there has to be one out-there idea in a business startup book!

Go to any part of the country and you will find a local or regional food for which the area is famous—a food that you are told you "must have" while you are there. Philly cheesesteak hoagie, Cincinnati chili, New England clam chowder, San Diego fish tacos, Maryland crabcakes, Buffalo wings, Chicago pizza, southern BBQ—every corner of the country has its own specialty.

The easy part is coming up with a long list of cultural foods. The hard part is figuring out what to do with that list. You would need to put your thinking cap on and be creative, but what could be more fun than trying to introduce the entire country to each other's cuisine?

There are any number of things you could do with "eating around America." A book, a recipe club, a restaurant that sells different specialty foods from around the country, delivery of regional foods from one part of the country to another—fresh lobsters are shipped all over the world, and what can be more difficult than that? Well, OK, the restaurant may be a little beyond the $5,000 limit of this book, but it would be a unique idea to work toward. Some items would be easy to ship ready-made, such as chowder, chili, frozen crabcakes, or even uncooked pizza.

THINGS TO CONSIDER

This is a business idea where you need to pull out all creative stops. What can you do to introduce culinary America to Joe Sixpack? The main thing to consider is that you will need to work very hard to figure it out. And you probably won't be able to get much financial support for your venture unless you really map out a solid plan.

HOW DO YOU WANT TO SPEND YOUR DAY?

How you would spend your day depends on what angle you take for this idea. You would need to spend considerable time lining up the vendors in the various parts of the country, if you plan to ship local foods.

WHAT YOU WILL NEED

You'll definitely need a computer and high-speed internet access to do research. From there, your needs depend on what you decide to do with the idea. You may need a shipping area and packing supplies. Or if you decide to just take orders and drop ship from the producers of the regional foods, you're computer will be key.

MARKETING ANGLE

One primary marketing angle you can take with this idea, if you decide to actually ship food, is to market to people in the area of the regional food to send something from "home" to that homesick child in college in California who would just love to taste a real Maryland crabcake or that son who moved from Buffalo to Florida for a great job, but would like nothing better than to have real Buffalo wings at his Super Bowl bash.

NICE TOUCH

Include coupons in your shipments, so the recipient can get more of their hometown foods whenever the yearning strikes. Or they can send the food to friends to taste what they've always been raving about.

EXPANSION POSSIBILITIES

Expansion possibilities are as simple as moving into one of the other suggested ideas for this business once the first one is off the ground. For instance, if you start with a cookbook, add shipping to your cultural foods idea.

WORDS TO KNOW

Drop ship: The process of having an order for a product made by another supplier and having the supplier ship the product directly to the person who ordered. It is useful because you don't have to carry inventory, and in the food industry it's essential not to have to ship fresh foods to a middleman who, in turn, then ships it to a customer.

Buffalo wings: A classic regional food originating in Buffalo, N.Y., these are chicken wings coated with a particular type of spicy barbecue sauce and served with celery and blue cheese dressing.

Whoopie pies: A New England confection consisting of a creamy filling sandwiched between two cake-like cookies.

RESOURCES

marylandcrabcakedelivery.com
whatscookingamerica.net

55 GREEN RESTAURANT CONSULTANT

Going "green" is a trend, not a fad. Every business wants to know how to be as environmentally friendly as possible, including restaurants. You can create a business that audits restaurants and provides them with a report on the things they can do to be more environmentally conscious.

There are many layers of a business that you can review for green changes. For instance:

- Check lighting. Are there places where incandescent bulbs could be replaced with compact fluorescents?

- Do an audit of the restaurant's electric appliances, from ovens to microwaves. Are they energy efficient? Are they older? If the restaurant upgrades, will they save in electrical or other fuel costs?

- Are there electric appliances that would be more efficient as gas-fired ones?

- What is the status of their heating and cooling systems? Are the units serviced annually to help keep them as efficient as possible? Is the building, or at least the space the restaurant occupies, well-insulated, including walls and windows?

- Does the restaurant find ways to compost their non-meat waste? This can be done with a special composting bin or by teaming up with a local farmer to provide scraps for pigs, goats, and/or chickens.

- Are paper, plastic, and other products recycled? Are the paper products they purchase made from recycled products themselves?

Does the restaurant attempt to minimize the amount of paper products they use, such as using cloth napkins or rationing systems for paper napkins?

- Has the restaurant found food sources for things such as free-range chicken and veal? Do they use products that are not tested on animals, including things such as the cleaning supplies used to clean the restaurant? Do they use only milk that is hormone-free?

- Do they have a policy on genetically altered produce?

- Is the restaurant using locally grown foods as much as possible?

- Do they employ other kinds of secondary "green" practices such as allowing their employees time off each year to do a community service or volunteer project? Or provide socially responsible investing options if they offer a company 401(k) plan?

THINGS TO CONSIDER

To be taken seriously in this occupation, you might want to get some training in something relevant to energy analysis, such as heating and cooling systems or even something like building inspection. You will need to learn as much as you can about things such as recycling, energy efficiency, alternative installations—anything about so-called "green" business practices.

HOW DO YOU WANT TO SPEND YOUR DAY?

Consulting to restaurants can provide for a very interesting workday. You will be spending some of your time doing actual audits, some of your time doing research, and some of your time marketing your services. And throw in a little continuing education throughout the year on a variety of projects.

WHAT YOU WILL NEED

You will definitely need a computer. For use on-site, you will want a laptop. Only you can decide if you are also comfortable using the laptop as your main computer in your office or if you also need a desktop. You might want both so that you can use your laptop on-site and for writing/storing the reports you generate. And as you write those reports, you can use your desktop as a reference tool to be able to research websites and information on the internet.

You will want to set up an office, although it doesn't have to be elaborate. A good computer work station, a fax machine, phone system, and some file storage are about all you should need. This can be in a separate room in your house or you could even carve out space in a corner of another room as long as you have the right furniture to stash everything away when you aren't using it.

MARKETING ANGLE

Your marketing angle will be to remind restaurants that they can use their "green" status for their own marketing. These days people want to know that companies are doing all that they can to help clean up and maintain the environment.

NICE TOUCH

Not only a nice touch, but one that is critical to your own marketing is that you uphold the same principles for yourself. For instance, make sure you use recycled paper for your reports and drive a fuel-efficient vehicle.

EXPANSION POSSIBILITIES

You can certainly expand to do green audits on other types of businesses. But before you do, become completely familiar with the restaurant industry.

Then move on to another industry, such as retail stores or office buildings. To become desirable as a consultant, you need a lot of expertise in one area before you are ready to apply it to another area.

WORDS TO KNOW

Compact fluorescent lightbulbs: A type of fluorescent lightbulb that uses approximately 75 percent less energy than incandescent bulbs and lasts 10 times longer, and is designed to fit into regular light fixtures.

Sustainability: The ability of a product or system to maintain a certain level of environmental integrity indefinitely. For instance, to have a "sustainable" woodlot would mean cutting only the amount of firewood each year as there are trees that would be grown to firewood size the next year.

RESOURCES

alliantenergy.com

eastcentralenergy.com

REFERENCES

UNITED STATES GOVERNMENT AGENCIES AND BUSINESS ASSOCIATIONS

Small Business Administration (SBA)

6302 Fairview Road, Suite 300
Charlotte, North Carolina 28210
Telephone: 800-827-5722   website: sba.gov
The U.S. Small Business Administration provides new entrepreneurs and existing business owners with financial, technical, and management resources to start, operate and grow a business. To find the local SBA office in your region, log onto sba.gov/regions/states.html.

SBA SERVICES AND PRODUCTS FOR ENTREPRENEURS

U.S. SBA Small Business Start-Up Guide

To order, contact your local SBA to order or log onto sba.gov/starting/indexstartup.html.

U.S. SBA Business Training Seminars and Courses

For more information, contact your local SBA office or log onto sba.gov/starting/indextraining.html.

U.S. SBA Business Plan; Road Map to Success

To order, contact your local SBA office or log onto sba.gov/starting/indexbusplans.html.

U.S. SBA Business Financing and Loan Programs

To order loan forms contact your local SBA office or log onto sba.gov/financing.

United States Department of Labor

Office of Small Business Programs (OSBP)

200 Constitution Avenue NW, Room C-2318

Washington, DC 20210

Telephone: 866-4-USA-DOL   website: dol.gov/osbp

OSBP promotes opportunities for small businesses, including small disadvantaged businesses, women-owned small businesses, HUBZone businesses, and businesses owned by service-disabled veterans.

United States Patent and Trademark Office

Commissioners of Patents and Trademarks

(Call or visit USPTO website for specific addresses.)

Telephone: 800-786-9199   website: uspto.gov

United States Copyright Office

Library of Congress

101 Independence Avenue SE

Washington, DC 20559-6000

Public Information Office: 202-707-3000

Forms and publications hotline: 202-707-9100   website: copyright.gov

The Internal Revenue Service (IRS)

Information for individuals: 800-829-1040

Information for businesses: 800-829-4933   website: irs.gov

Federal and business tax information from the source.

Service Corps of Retired Executives (SCORE)

409 Third Street SW, 6th Floor

Washington, DC 20024

Telephone: 800-634-0245   website: score.org

SCORE is a nonprofit association in partnership with the Small Business Administration that provides aspiring entrepreneurs and business owners with free business counseling and mentoring programs. It consists of more than 11,000 volunteer business counselors in 389 regional chapters located throughout the U.S. They have helped over 7.2 million small businesses.

U.S. Chamber of Commerce

1615 H Street NW

Washington, DC 20062-2000

Telephone: 202-659-6000

Customer Service: 800-638-6582   website: uschamber.com

The U.S. Chamber of Commerce represents small businesses, corporations, and trade associations from coast to coast. Call 202-659-6000 or log onto their website to locate a regional branch.

United States Association for Small Businesses and Entrepreneurship

DeSantis Center, Suite 207

Florida Atlantic University-College of Business

777 Glades Road, Boca Raton, FL 33431-0992

Telephone: 561-297-4060   website: usasbe.org

An affiliate of the International Council for Small Business, the USASBE is established to advance knowledge and business education through seminars, conferences, white papers, and various programs.

National Business Incubation Association (NBIA)

20 E. Circle Drive, #37198

Athens, OH 45701-3571

Telephone: 704-593-4331   website: nbia.org

In the U.S. there are more than 900 business incubation programs, and NBIA provides links to them. Additionally, NBIA assists entrepreneurs with information, education, and networking resources to help in the early development stages of business start-up and the advanced stages of business growth.

National Business Association

P.O. Box 700728

Dallas, Texas 75370

Telephone: 800-456-0440   website: nationalbusiness.org

This nonprofit association assists self-employed individuals and small business owners by using group buying power to provide health plans, educational opportunities and other valuable services.

National Association of Women Business Owners (NAWBO)

8405 Greensboro Drive, Suite #800

McLean, VA 22102

Telephone: 800-55-NAWBO   website: nawbo.org

NAWBO provides women business owner members with support, resources, and business information to help grow and prosper in their own businesses.

UMass Amherst Family Business Center

Continuing and Professional Education

100 Venture Way, Suite 201

Hadley, MA 01035

Telephone: 413-545-1537   website: umass.edu/fambiz/

UMass Family Business Center provides members with training programs, information, and workshops to assist with building entrepreneurial skills that can be best utilized in a family-owned and operated business.

National Association for the Self-Employed (NASE)

P.O. Box 612067 DFW Airport

Dallas, TX 75261-2067

Telephone: 800-232-6273   website: nase.org

Founded in 1981, NASE is an organization whose members include small business owners and professionals who are self-employed. NASE provides members with support, education, and training to help them succeed and prosper in business.

National Small Business Association (NSBA)

1156 15th Street NW, Suite 1100

Washington, D.C. 20005

Telephone: 800-345-6728   website: nsba.biz

A volunteer-based agency that focuses on small business advocacy in an effort to promote federal policies of benefit to small businesses and the growth of free enterprise. Since 1937, NSBA has grown from representing 160 small businesses to representing over 150,000.

International Franchise Association (IFA)

1501 K Street, N.W., Suite 350

Washington, D.C. 20005

Telephone: 202-628-8000   website: franchise.org

IFA membership organization includes franchisers, franchisees, and service and product suppliers for the franchising industry.

BUSINESS BOOKS AND PUBLICATIONS

Suggested Reading

The 30 Second Commute: The Ultimate Guide to Starting and Operating a Home-Based Business, Beverley Williams and Don Cooper, New York: McGraw-Hill, 2004

101+ Answers to the Most Frequently Asked Questions From Entrepreneurs, Courtney H. Price, New York: John Wiley & Sons, 1999.

303 Marketing Tips: Guaranteed to Boost Your Business!, Rieva Lesonsky and Leann Anderson, Irvine, CA: Entrepreneur Press, 1999.

Ben Franklin's 12 Rules of Management: The Founding Father of American Business Solves Your Toughest Business Problems, Blaine McCormick, Irvine, CA: Entrepreneur Press, 2000.

The Best Home Businesses for the 21st Century: The Inside Information You Need to Know to Select a Home-Based Business That's Right for You, Paul and Sarah Edwards, Los Angeles, CA: J.P Tarcher, 1999.

The Book of Entrepreneurs' Wisdom: Classic Writings by Legendary Entrepreneurs, Peter Krass, New York: John Wiley & Sons, 1999.

Business Plans Made Easy: It's Not as Hard as You Think!, Mark Henricks, Irvine, CA: Entrepreneur Press, 1999.

The Complete Idiot's Guide to Starting a Home-Based Business, Second Edition, Barbara Weltman and Beverly Williams, Indianapolis, IN: Alpha Books, 2000.

The Customer Revolution, Patricia B. Seybold, New York: Crown Publishing, 2001.

E-Service: 24 Ways to Keep Your Customers When the Competition is Just a Click Away, Ron Zemke and Thomas K. Connellan, New York: AMACOM, 2000.

The Entrepreneur Next Door, Bill Wagner, Irvine, CA: Entrepreneur Press, 2006.

The Entrepreneur's Internet Handbook: Your Legal and Practical Guide to Starting a Business Website, Hugo Barreca and Julia K. O'Neill, Naperville, IL: Sourcebooks, 2002.

Entrepreneur's Toolkit: Tools and Techniques to Launch and Grow Your New Business (Harvard Business Essentials), Richard Luecke, Harvard Business School Press, 2004.

Food Booth: The Complete Guide to Starting and Operating a Food Concession Stand, Barbara J. Fitzgerald, Carnival Press, 2006.

From Kitchen to Market: Selling Your Gourmet Food Specialty, Stephen Hall, Kaplan Business, 2005.

The Girl's Guide to Starting Your Own Business: Candid Advice, Frank Talk, and True Stories for the Successful Entrepreneur, Caitlin Friedman and Kimberly Yorio, Collins, 2004.

Grow Your Business, Mark Henricks, Irvine, CA: Entrepreneur Press, 2001.

How To Dotcom: A Step-by-Step Guide to e-Commerce, Robert McGarvey, Irvine, CA: Entrepreneur Press, 2000.

How to Open a Financially Successful Bakery (with CD), Sharon Fullen and Douglas R. Brown, Atlantic Publishing Company, 2004.

How to Open a Financially Successful Coffee, Espresso, & Tea Shoppe, Elizabeth Godsmark, Laurie Arduser, Douglas R. Brown.

If at First You Don't Succeed... : The Eight Patterns of Highly Effective Entrepreneurs, Brent Bowers, New York: Currency, 2006.

Import/Export: How to Get Started in International Trade, Carl A. Nelson, New York: McGraw-Hill, 2000.

Knock Out Marketing: Powerful Strategies to Punch Up Your Sales, Jack Ferreri, Irvine, CA: Entrepreneur Press, 1999.

Legal Guide For Starting & Running A Small Business (8th Edition), Fred S. Steingold and Ilona M. Bray, Berkeley, CA: NOLO, 2005.

Masters of Success, Ivan R. Misner and Don Morgan, Irvine, CA: Entrepreneur Press, 2005.

Permission Based E-Mail Marketing That Works!, Kim MacPherson and Rosalind Resnick, Chicago: Dearborn Trade, 2001.

Positioning: The Battle for Your Mind, Al Ries and Jack Trout, New York: McGraw-Hill, 2001.

Public Relations Kit for Dummies, Eric Yaverbaum and Bill Bly, Foster City, CA: Hungry Minds Inc., 2001.

Six-Week Start-Up: A Step-By-Step Program for Starting Your Business, Making Money, and Achieving Your Goals!, Rhonda Abrams, Palo Alto, CA: Planning Shop, 2004.

Start Your Own Business, Rieva Lesonsky, Irvine, CA: Entrepreneur Press, 2001.

Start Your Own Business: The Only Start-Up Book You'll Ever Need, Rieva Lesonsky, Irvine, CA: Entrepreneur Press, Third Edition, 2004.

Start Your Own Restaurant and Five Other Food Businesses, Jacquelyn Lynn, Irvine, CA: Entrepreneur Press, 2006.

Start Your Own Senior Services Business, Jacquelyn Lynn and Charlene Davis, Irvine, CA: Entrepreneur Press, 2006.

Start Your Restaurant Career, Heather Heath Dismore, Irvine, CA: Entrepreneur Press, 2006.

Starting on a Shoestring: Building a Business Without a Bankroll, Arnold S. Goldstein, New York: John Wiley & Sons, 2002.

Straight Talk About Starting and Growing Your Business, Sanjyot P. Dunung, New York: McGraw-Hill, 2005.

Successful Business Planning in 30 Days: A Step-By-Step Guide for Writing a Business Plan and Starting Your Own Business, Third Edition, Peter J. Patsula, Petsula Media, 2004.

Think Big: Nine Ways to Make Millions From Your Ideas, Don Debelak, Irvine, CA: Entrepreneur Press, 2001.

Time Tested Advertising Methods, John Caples and Fred E. Hahn, Upper Saddle River, NJ: Prentice Hall, 1998.

The Way to the Top: The Best Business Advice I Ever Received, Donald Trump, New York: Crown Business, 2004.

Unofficial Guide to Starting a Business Online, Jason R. Rich, New York: John Wiley & Sons, 2006.

The Unofficial Guide to Starting a Small Business, Marcia Layton Turner, New York: John Wiley & Sons, 2004.

Where's the Money? Sure-Fire Financing Solutions for Your Small Business, Art Beroff and Dwayne Moyers, Irvine, CA: Entrepreneur Media Inc., 1999.

MAGAZINES

e-Business Advisor, Advisor Media Inc., P.O. Box 429002, San Diego, CA 92142-9002. 858-278-5600, advisor.com

Business Week, The McGraw-Hill Companies, P.O. Box 182604, Columbus, OH 43272. 877-833-5524, businessweek.com

Entrepreneur, Entrepreneur Media Inc., 2445 McCabe Way, Irvine, CA 92614. 800-274-6229, entrepreneur.com

Family Business, Family Business Publishing Company, 1845 Walnut Street, Suite 900, Philadelphia, PA 19103. 800-637-4464, familybusinessmagazine.com

Fast Company, Forbes, 90 5th Avenue, New York, NY 10011. 800-295-0893, forbes.com

Franchise Times, 2808 Anthony Lane, S. Mpls, MN 55418. 800-528-3296, franchisetimes.com

Inc., 100 First Avenue, 4th Floor, Building 36, Charlestown, MA 02129. 800-234-0999, inc.com

Marketers Forum, Forum Publishing Company, 383 E. Main Street, Centerport, NY 11721. 800-635-7654, forum123.com

Opportunity World and *Money 'N Profits,* United Communication, 130 Church St. #257, NY, NY 10007. Telephone: 212-786-0291, oppworld.com

Promo, P.O. Box 10587, Riverton, NJ 08076-8575. 800-775-3777, promomagazine.com

SMALL BUSINESS SOFTWARE

Business Plan Pro
Palo Alto Software
The Standard version comes with more than 500 business plans and more than 9,000 industry profiles, while the Premier version adds collaboration tools and business valuation analysis. Both are designed to help launch entrepreneurs on their way to tremendous success.

Business Plan Pro: eBay Edition
Palo Alto Software
As eBay has grown into a unique home for thousands of businesses, the need for specialized business plans has emerged. This special edition includes eBay-specific examples, sales forecasts and more.

Marketing Plan Pro
Palo Alto Software
From the initial budget breakdown and spreadsheets to the final marketing plan, this software has the necessary tools to implement a marketing strategy and put together a top-notch plan for any size business.

Microsoft Office Small Business Accounting
Microsoft
Designed for Windows XP, Small Business Accounting helps the owner, manager or bookkeeper handle all financial matters from tracking inventory and payroll to putting together all necessary financial reports.

Microsoft Office Small Business Management Edition 2006
Microsoft

Also designed for Windows XP, Business Management helps business owners and managers keep track of sales information, cash flow, invoices and the numerous details of running a company.

QuickBooks Pro 2009

Intuit Inc.

Mac and PC versions offer a wide range of financial and accounting options that allow you to track sales and expenses, pay bills, handle payroll, track inventory and create estimates and reports for small or homebased businesses. The programs are designed to easily interface with many PC or Mac programs as necessary.

Quicken Premier Home & Business 2009

Intuit Inc.

Easy-to-navigate financial software for home and small businesses as well as self-employed professionals. The PC-based program is designed to handle all common business billing and tax basics while helping you monitor expenses and keep tabs on assets. The Mac version is also very popular and helps small business professionals manage cash, pay bills, and handle additional financial details.

INTERNET AND E-COMMERCE RESOURCES

All Business

allbusiness.com

You'll find numerous articles and plenty of tips and information in the Advice Center at this very comprehensive web business center. You can also search articles from 700 business periodicals, download business forms or check out numerous business guides and directories.

Bplans

Bplans.com

Expert advice, business planning tools, and many sample business plans for numerous types of businesses are available from Bplans.com. Articles, expert advices, resources, and software are all part of this comprehensive site.

Entrepreneur Online

entrepreneur.com

This is your one-stop source for small business information, products, and services online. View current articles from *Entrepreneur* magazine, get expert advice for all your small business questions, and browse through the thousands of small business and franchise opportunities featured on the site. It's all there in one convenient location that has been specifically developed to help entrepreneurs start, run, and grow their small businesses.

Cafepress.com

cafepress.com

Cafepress lets you build a store for your website that features promotional products such as T-shirts and hats with your company logo or message emblazoned on them. They are unique in that they create your products at their site and ship the products directly to your online customers. No costly inventory to purchase. Cafepress does it all for you and you keep a portion of the profits from every sale.

CNNMoney

cnnmoney.com

The markets, business news, and plenty of articles on personal finance, real estate and, of course, small business highlight this major site from CNN, designed to keep readers on top of the latest financial news. The Small Business section includes articles, newsletters, podcasts, and calculators. The latest in small business news is updated regularly to help you stay on top of the currency industry trends and economic factors.

MerchantExpress.com

merchantexpress.com

Merchant Express provides internet entrepreneurs, homebased business owners, and retail storefront owners merchant accounts and credit card processing options and solutions. Increase revenues and improve customer services by providing your customers with credit card payment options.

My Own Business

myownbusiness.org

An online course on starting a business, originally developed as a bricks-and-mortar business after the California riots in 1992. A free 14-session course is offered, plus an $85 certified course and textbook. The site also offers a range of resources, business term glossary, and more.

Nolo.com

nolo.com

This is a one-stop source for online law information and legal forms pertaining to small business, employees, trademarks, and copyrights. If it has to do with the law, you will find it here. This site is large, easy to navigate, and jam-packed full of legal advice, books, forms, software and information.

Startup Journal

startupjournal.com

The Wall Street Journal Center for Entrepreneurs includes leading columnists, plus articles on financing, e-commerce and various new business ideas. You can also find businesses and franchises for sale and various business opportunities plus a well-stocked business bookstore and much more.

RESOURCES IN THIS BOOK

abouteating.com

acitydiscount.com

alliantenergy.com

allrecipes.com

anoccasionalchocolate.com

americastestkitchen.com

angelfire.com

apppa.org

artisancheesefestival.com

artistshelpingchildren.org

ascateringsupplies.com

atticshoppe.com

bajafishtacos.net

bartending.org

bartending.com

basket4picnic.com

bbqadvisor.com

bbqgalore.com

boba.com

breadtopia.com

breworganic.com

bubbleteasupply.com

burford.com

cafemom.com

cakerysupplies.com

campusdeliveryassociates.com

carriageworks.com

cartsandgrills.com

catchannel.com

cateringsupplies.com

ccof.org

ces.ncsu.edu/depts/hort/hil/hil-8110.html

coffeecow.com

containerandpackaging.com

cookspalate.com

cookware.org

cowboyfreerangemeat.com

culinarybusiness.com

culinarycafe.com

delivery.com

dinewise.com

dinnersdone.net

eastcentralenergy.com

eatright.org

ebay.com

ediblearrangements.com

ehow.com/how_2054510_
    teach-cooking-class.html

elementsoftaste.com

ellenskitchen.com

farmersmarket.com

fda.gov

festivities-pub.com

foodnetwork.com

foodshedalliance.org

ftd.com

fullerssugarhouse.com

gardenguides.com

garden.org

giftwarenews.com

healthrecipes.com

healthysmoothierecipe.net

hireachef.com

jameshaller.com

kinderinfo.com

leaseithere.com

littlewoodfarm.org

localcookingclass.com

makeicecream.com

maplesyrupsupplies.com

marylandcrabcakedelivery.com

mastercraftprinting.com

midwestorganic.com

mikitchenessukitchen.com

mitechtrading.com

mycleaningproducts.com

mymommybiz.com/ideas/cookingclass.
   html

northeastwinemaking.com

northernpizzaequipment.com

nutsite.com

nutsonline.com

Olympiafood.coop

onestopcandle.com

organicconsumers.org

organicgardening.com

pastabiz.com

personalchef.com

picnicsupplyworld.com

placematprinters.com

popcornsupply.com

popsezpopcorn.com

pretzeltime.com

pumpkinridgegardens.com

putneycoop.com

recipetips.com

recipezaar.com

restaurantguide.com

restaurant.org

restaurantrow.com

salsa-recipes.com

sandjcatering.net

seafoodbusiness.com

simplybabyfoodrecipes.com

solutionsforseafood.com

sheepdairying.com

simply-elegant-cakes.com

southernconcessionsupply.com

streetvendor.netfirms.com

supremeproducts.com

tea-and-coffee.com

testkitchens.com

thefruitpages.com

toolcrib.com

travellinggourmet.com

vendingtrucks.com

webstaurantstore.com

webtender.com

wegoshop.com

whatscookingamerica.net

whfoods.com

wholesalejanitorialsupply.com

winemakinginfo-online.com

woodworkingtools.com

woodworkersworkshop.com

writers-publish.com

INDEX

Insurance coverage, 9
Internet service, 11–12

J

Juice drinks, 108–111
  expansion possibilities, 110
  how do you want to spend your day?, 109
  marketing angle, 109–110
  nice touch, 110
  overview, 108
  preparing the drinks, 108
  recipes, 108
  resources, 111
  selling your drinks, 108–109
  things to consider, 109
  what you will need, 109
  words to know, 110–111

K

Kitchen incubator, 216–218
  expansion possibilities, 218
  how do you want to spend your day?, 217
  marketing angle, 217
  nice touch, 217–218
  overview, 216
  resources, 218
  things to consider, 217
  what you will need, 217
  words to know, 218

L

Labeling
  and packaging, 2–3
  ingredient, 4
Licensing requirements, 2
Liquor commission, 2
Lunch wagon, 77–81
  expansion possibilities, 80–81
  how do you want to spend your day?, 79
  marketing angle, 79–80
  nice touch, 80
  overview, 77–78
  resources, 81
  things to consider, 79

what you will need, 79
words to know, 81

M

Maple syrup production/sales, 42–46
  expansion possibilities, 46
  how do you want to spend your day?, 44
  marketing angle, 45–46
  nice touch, 46
  overview, 42–44
  resources, 46
  things to consider, 44
  what you will need, 45
  words to know, 46
Meals-to-go, 58–61
  customer pick-up, 59
  expansion possibilities, 60
  how do you want to spend your day?, 59
  marketing angle, 60
  nice touch, 60
  overview, 58
  resources, 61
  things to consider, 59
  words to know, 61

N

Nut sales, 166–169
  expansion possibilities, 168–169
  how do you want to spend your day?, 167
  marketing angle, 168
  nice touch, 168
  overview, 166
  resources, 169
  things to consider, 166–167
  what you will need, 167
  words to know, 169

O

Office equipment, 10–13
Overview, industry, 1–13

P

Pasta, fresh, 112–115
  expansion possibilities, 115